MacBook Air 2024 User's Guide

A Detailed Manual for Beginners and Seniors to unlock the Hidden Features and Functions of the New Apple 13-inch and 15-inch M3 MacBook Air 2024

Perry

Hoover

Disclaimer

The information in this book is based on personal experience and anecdotal evidence. Although the author has made every attempt to achieve an accuracy of the information gathered in this book, they make no representation or warranties concerning the accuracy or completeness of the contents of this book. Your circumstances may not be suited to some illustrations in this book.

The author disclaims any liability arising directly or indirectly from the use of this book. Readers are encouraged to seek Medical. Accounting, legal, or professional help when required.

This guide is for informational purposes only, and the author does not accept any responsibilities for any liabilities resulting from the use of this information. While every attempt has been made to verify the information provided here, the author cannot assume any responsibility for errors, inaccuracies or omission.

Printed in the United States of America

Table of Contents

INTRODUCTION

Apple has recently unveiled its latest additions to the MacBook Air lineup, introducing the highly anticipated 13-inch and 15-inch models powered by the cutting-edge Apple M3 chip. The announcement has generated significant excitement in the tech community, as these top-tier laptops promise to deliver exceptional performance and functionality. With anticipation reaching its peak, consumers are eager to explore the innovative features and advancements offered by these new MacBook Air models.

The Apple M3 chip, which made its debut late last year, has already garnered attention for its remarkable capabilities demonstrated in the latest MacBook Pro models and the iMac 24-inch. As such, there are high expectations for the performance of the M3-powered MacBook Air models. The chip's integration into the MacBook Air lineup signifies Apple's commitment to pushing the boundaries of technological innovation and providing users with state-of-the-art computing experiences.

Now that the latest MacBook Air models are here, it's time to delve into all the essential details surrounding these upgrades. From enhanced specifications to innovative features, Apple has undoubtedly packed these laptops with impressive functionalities designed to meet the needs of modern users. Whether it's improved processing power, enhanced graphics performance, or extended battery life, these MacBook Air models are poised to deliver an unparalleled user experience.

In addition to highlighting the new features and specifications of the MacBook Air models, it's crucial to provide users with valuable tips and tricks to navigate these devices seamlessly. From optimizing performance to maximizing productivity, understanding how to leverage the capabilities of these laptops can significantly enhance the overall user experience. Whether it's mastering the latest macOS features or unlocking hidden functionalities, users can benefit from expert guidance to make the most out of their MacBook Air.

CHAPTER ONE

M3 13-inch New Features

Price & availability

The 13-inch MacBook Air (M3) was introduced to the public on March 4, 2024, and pre-orders for the device were made available through Apple's online shop beginning on the same day. On March 8, it formally made its debut in retail establishments.

An M3 chip with an 8-core central processing unit (CPU), an 8-core graphics processing unit (GPU), 8GB of unified memory, and 256GB of solid-state drive (SSD) storage is included in the base model, which has a price tag of $1,099, £1,099, or AU$1,799, respectively. This M3 chip is identical to the one that is found in the base iMac 24-inch (M3), which has a starting price of $1,399, 1,399, or 2,199 Australian dollars. This is a considerable increase in price for the all-in-one personal computer.

You also have the option of purchasing the MacBook Air 13-inch (M3), which comes with a more powerful 35W dual USB-C power adapter (in comparison to the standard model's 30W adapter) and costs $1,299, £1,299, or AU$2,099, and features an 8-core central processing unit (CPU), a 10-core graphics processing unit (GPU), 8GB of unified memory, and 512GB of solid-state drive (SSD) storage.

A pre-configured MacBook Air 13-inch (M3) with the same M3 processor and specifications is available for $1,499, £1,499, or AU$2,399, and it comes with 16GB of unified memory and 512GB of solid-state storage. This model is designed for individuals who are interested in achieving higher levels of performance. Here, we are going to look at this particular model.

In the same way that its predecessors were able to be further personalized, the new MacBook Air can be further configured with up to 24GB of unified memory, 2TB of solid-state storage, and a 70W USB-C power converter. Priced at $2,299 / £2,299 / AU$3,599, the fully maxed-out model is available for purchase.

There is a notable difference between the M2 MacBook Air and the M3 MacBook Air in terms of the price of the base model when it was first introduced. The M2 model was initially made available for purchase in 2022, and the base model was priced at $1,199, £1,249, or AU$1,899. Despite the fact that the M2 model has now been reduced by $100 in price, the fact that it was initially priced so high was a source of dispute. The fact that Apple is addressing this issue with the M3 model, which provides a better value for the money, is quite encouraging.

Furthermore, Apple will continue to provide the 13-inch MacBook Air with M2, which is currently priced at $999, £999, or $1,599 in Australia. This action is reminiscent to the method that was used during the introduction of the M2 MacBook Air, in which the M1 model continued to be offered at the lower price point of $999.

Customers are now able to get the superior M2 MacBook Air at a price that is more appealing to them as a result of this decision. On the other hand, this also indicates that Apple will no longer be selling the M1 design. Despite this, other vendors are already selling the M1 model at rates that are even lower than the MSRP. This is because they are trying to clear out their inventory in preparation for the release of the new MacBook Airs.

It is recommended that individuals who are looking for the most cost-effective choice that comes directly from Apple purchase the M2 MacBook Air. On the other hand, the M3 model provides an outstanding value for the money and is currently the most reasonably priced Mac that is powered by the M3 processor. This will remain the case until the planned release of an M3-powered Mac mini in the near future.

Specs

The Apple MacBook Air 13-inch (M3) offers three pre-configured options, with the flexibility to customize memory and storage before purchase to align with the review and max configurations outlined below.

MacBook Air 13-inch (M3) Configurations:

1. **Base Configuration**:
   - Price: $1,399 / £1,399 / AU$2,199

- CPU: Apple M3 (8-core)
- Graphics: Integrated 8-core GPU
- RAM: 8GB unified memory
- Storage: 256GB SSD
- Screen: 13.6-inch, 2560 x 1664 Liquid Retina display (500 nits sustained brightness, wide color P3 gamut, True Tone technology)
- Ports: 2x Thunderbolt 4 (USB-C), 3.5mm headphone jack, MagSafe 3
- Wireless: Wi-Fi 6E (802.11ax), Bluetooth 5.3
- Camera: 1080p FaceTime HD webcam
- Weight: 2.7 lbs (1.24kg)
- Dimensions: 11.97 x 8.46 x 0.44 inches (304 x 215 x 11.3mm)

2. **Review Configuration:**

- Price: $1,499 / £1,499 / AU$2,399
- CPU: Apple M3 (8-core)
- Graphics: Integrated 10-core GPU
- RAM: 16GB unified memory
- Storage: 512GB SSD

- Screen: 13.6-inch, 2560 x 1664 Liquid Retina display (500 nits sustained brightness, wide color P3 gamut, True Tone technology)
- Ports: 2x Thunderbolt 4 (USB-C), 3.5mm headphone jack, MagSafe 3
- Wireless: Wi-Fi 6E (802.11ax), Bluetooth 5.3
- Camera: 1080p FaceTime HD webcam
- Weight: 2.7 lbs (1.24kg)
- Dimensions: 11.97 x 8.46 x 0.44 inches (304 x 215 x 11.3mm)

3. Max Configuration:

- Price: $2,299 / £2,299 / AU$3,599
- CPU: Apple M3 (8-core)
- Graphics: Integrated 10-core GPU
- RAM: 24GB unified memory
- Storage: 2TB SSD
- Screen: 13.6-inch, 2560 x 1664 Liquid Retina display (500 nits sustained brightness, wide color P3 gamut, True Tone technology)

- Ports: 2x Thunderbolt 4 (USB-C), 3.5mm headphone jack, MagSafe 3
- Wireless: Wi-Fi 6E (802.11ax), Bluetooth 5.3
- Camera: 1080p FaceTime HD webcam
- Weight: 2.7 lbs (1.24kg)
- Dimensions: 11.97 x 8.46 x 0.44 inches (304 x 215 x 11.3mm)

Review and Recommendations:

The base configuration with 8GB of memory and 256GB SSD might feel outdated for the price, particularly for tasks involving multiple applications or creative work such as photo or video editing. Considering the limited upgrade options and the weaker integrated GPU, it's advisable to invest in the review configuration for better future-proofing, with 16GB of memory and a 512GB SSD.

Design

Even though the Apple MacBook Air 13-inch (M3) does not feature any revolutionary shifts in its design, it is not necessary for it to do so. We had a lot of affection for the M1 MacBook Air, but its design had started to show signs of its advanced age. The M2 MacBook, which was released by Apple in 2022, featured a stunning overhaul that included a screen that was both upgraded and larger, bezels that were considerably thinner, and an overall appearance that was very contemporary. The fact that the M3 MacBook Air and its predecessor have a similar appearance is not anything that bothers me from a personal standpoint because I was pleased with the redesign.

In spite of this, this laptop continues to be a remarkable example of sleekness and minimal weight. The LED display measures 13.6 inches and features a brightness and vibrancy that is impressive. Additionally, its native resolution of 2560 x 1664 pixels provides a clear and detailed image with 224 pixels per inch. The 15-inch MacBook Air (M3), which was released concurrently with the 13-inch model, is similar to its predecessor in that it has a larger screen with a better resolution, which results in a pixel density that is comparable to that of the 13-inch model.

To put it simply, the visual quality will not be compromised in any way, regardless of the model of MacBook Air that you choose to purchase. Because of its lighter and more compact form, the 13-inch model will provide higher levels of convenience for a large number of users, while yet maintaining a high level of capability. For a device that is so compact, the keyboard manages to keep its pleasant feel while still providing a surprisingly significant amount of key travel. The keyboard of the MacBook Air has a haptic and responsive feel to it as you type on it. On top of that, the incorporation of a Touch ID button makes it possible to quickly turn the device on and to log in using fingerprint identification without any difficulty.

In terms of connections, the MacBook Air M3 keeps the same configuration as its predecessor. It has two Thunderbolt 3/USB 4 ports that are capable of transferring data at a rate of up to 40 gigabytes per second, in addition to a MagSafe 3 port for charging and a 3.5mm headphone socket.

On the other hand, it is important to point out that the MagSafe 3 and Thunderbolt ports are located on the left side of the device. This may be a source of annoyance when using several peripherals at the same time. A further disadvantage of this configuration is that it prevents the user from selecting which side of the charger to plug in. In spite of this, customers are able to charge the smartphone using USB-C chargers manufactured by other brands even if the MagSafe port is not present.

Not a single one of the new MacBook Air models is compatible with Thunderbolt 4, which is a crucial point to address. Those Macs that are equipped with M3 Pro and M3 Max chips are the only ones that can access this capability.

The upgrade to M3 also makes it possible for the new MacBook Air 13-inch to support twin external monitors concurrently. One of the panels can support up to 6K resolution at 60Hz, while the other monitor can support up to 5K resolution. This is in contrast to the earlier M2 model, which could only support a single external monitor with a resolution of 6K.

However, it is important to remember that there is a big limitation: turning off the lid of the MacBook Air is required in order to use two external monitors. When you open the lid, one of the external screens will become inactive, which means that you will not be able to use all three screens at the same time. Despite the fact that this may not be a problem for office workers who normally use their laptops in a closed-lid setting with a dock, the execution is a little bit cumbersome. It is interesting to note that the MacBook Pro 14-inch with the M3 chip was first released without this functionality; however, Apple intends to enable it through a software update in the near future.

In general, the MacBook Air 13-inch (M3) continues Apple's heritage of producing a notebook that is both streamlined and lightweight. Despite the fact that it is quite similar to its predecessor, it yet emanates a sense of refinement and contemporaryness.

Although the new MacBook Air is "almost identical," the phrase "almost identical" is not totally accurate. The "breakthrough anodization seal" featured on the Midnight color variation is designed to reduce the amount of fingerprints that are left on the device. When compared to the previous model in the same color, which had a tendency to show and keep fingerprints, scratches, and other marks, this model addresses the issues that were made against it.

Even though the 13-inch MacBook Air that was provided for evaluation was in the Starlight color (with other color possibilities including Midnight, Space Gray, and Silver), I had the opportunity to take a quick look at a Midnight 13-inch MacBook Air that was sitting in Apple's offices in London. Upon initial inspection, it seems that the new Midnight finish is actually more resistant to fingerprints than its predecessor.

Apple also highlights the fact that the new MacBook Air is the company's first product to integrate recycled materials to the extent of fifty percent. A hundred percent recycled aluminum is used for the body, while one hundred percent recycled copper is used for the main logic board. A greater degree of adaptability in terms of enabling consumers to repair or upgrade products would be greatly appreciated; nonetheless, any improvement in the utilization of recycled materials is a step in the right direction.

Performance

The M3 chip, which is Apple's most modern silicon and was debuted alongside the most recent MacBook Pros, is included into the new MacBook Air 13-inch, which is the most notable aspect of this update. In contrast to the MacBook Pros that were released the previous year, the MacBook Air 13-inch is the only model that uses the M3 chip. It does not include the M3 Pro or M3 Max variations, which are more powerful. Due to the fact that the MacBook Air is more appealing to users from the general public, it is highly improbable that it will be used for heavy-duty creative jobs.

There are two variants of the M3 CPU that are available for the Apple MacBook Air 13-inch: the base model, which comes with an 8-core graphics processing unit (GPU), and a slightly upgraded version that has a 10-core GPU. An eight-core central processing unit (CPU) that is dynamically regulated by the MacBook Air to improve performance and battery life is included in both types of the MacBook Air. This CPU consists of four high-performance cores and four efficiency cores.

The Apple MacBook Air 13-inch (M3) has the capability of being configured with up to 24GB of unified memory and 2TB of solid-state drive storage, according to the specifications. The evaluation device that was provided for testing consists of a 10-core M3 CPU, 16 gigabytes of memory, and 512 gigabytes of storage space. It's possible that selecting the base model won't result in the same level of performance, although it's anticipated that the difference would be rather minor.

In spite of this, it is recommended to go with a MacBook Air that has a larger memory and storage capacity. This is especially true when taking into consideration the fact that 8 gigabytes of random access memory (RAM) and 256 gigabytes of solid-state drive (SSD) can seem like a limitation for a laptop in the year 2024. Especially obvious with the 256GB variant is the fact that the pre-installed macOS and applications take a sizeable chunk of the available storage space.

The Apple MacBook Air 13-inch (M3) performs exceptionally well in real-world testing. The rapid responsiveness of macOS Sonoma is backed by an expanding selection of applications that are tuned for Apple's M series CPUs, which allows the operating system to fully leverage the capabilities of the hardware. The performance is consistent across a wide range of activities, from simple surfing on Safari to more demanding applications such as Adobe Photoshop.

Apple's M-series CPUs are noteworthy for their efficiency, which results in little heat generation. This is one of the advantages of these chips. When combined with Apple's thermal architecture, the MacBook Air 13-inch (M3) is able to function without the need of fans, resulting in a silent operation. This absence of fan noise is especially beneficial for audio recording since it guarantees a pristine recording environment that is free from background interruptions. This is a significant difference from the regular fan activity that is observed with many Windows laptops.

When it comes to the built-in features, the new MacBook Air with a 13-inch screen has a three-mic array that improves clarity and reduces interference from ambient noise. Additionally, the FaceTime HD camera keeps its 1080p resolution. Notably, in a world where many laptops in this price bracket still use 720p webcams, Apple's inclusion of a high-quality camera is praiseworthy. This is especially true in light of the increased emphasis on video conversations and meetings in both professional and social realms since the beginning of the pandemic.

Apple maintains that the M3 chip is responsible for the improvement in the quality of both the audio and video. In spite of the fact that I did not notice any differences when compared to the M2 MacBook Air, which has the same webcam and microphone configuration, the results are still crisp and clear.

In addition, the M3 MacBook Air features improved Wi-Fi compatibility, which is now compatible with Wi-Fi 6E (in contrast to the Wi-Fi 6 variant that was previously available). This allows for faster speeds and more stable connections over wider distances. The wireless connectivity of the MacBook Air 13-inch (M3) proved to be great in my experience with the device.

In addition, the MacBook Air 13-inch (M3) demonstrates respectable performance in contemporary gaming, even being able to handle some games that are graphically demanding enough to be considered satisfactory. Although it may not be able to compete with top-tier gaming laptops, the potential of gaming on a MacBook Air that is both compact and lightweight is now a possibility, which was a vision that appeared to be almost impossible in the past. On the bright 13.6-inch display, the games I examined were fairly impressive, despite the fact that there were limitations attached to pushing the visual settings to their greatest limits. The absence of fans on the MacBook Air provides a novel gaming experience for a person who plays video games on a personal computer. This is a departure from the cumbersome and noisy gaming laptops that are generally associated with the gaming scene.

People's attention was brought to the fact that Apple places a strong emphasis on its artificial intelligence capabilities after the company announced the new MacBook Air 13-inch (M3). A pleasant surprise was Apple's decision to prioritize artificial intelligence performance on the MacBook Air 13-inch (M3). This decision came at a time when artificial intelligence, and more specifically content generation, is receiving a lot of attention. Apple has maintained a lead in artificial intelligence capabilities over its competitors, such as Microsoft and Google, ever since the first M1 chip was introduced. This has been made possible by the incorporation of the Apple Neural Engine.

The MacBook Air is positioned as "the world's best consumer laptop for artificial intelligence" according to Apple, thanks to the enhanced 16-core Neural Engine that is included in the M3 CPU. My observations of the MacBook Air 13-inch (M3) handling cloud-based and on-device AI tasks were outstanding, despite the fact that it is difficult to provide evidence to support this claim until additional laptops equipped with chips that are focused on artificial intelligence are commercially available.

There are higher-end options available, such as the MacBook Pro, which offer mini LED technology and ProMotion features for enhanced contrast, vibrancy, and smoother scrolling. Despite the fact that the screen and speakers may not represent the pinnacle of MacBook technology, the 13-inch MacBook Air (M3) still delivers commendable performance.

The inclusion of four speakers, which are not as advanced as the six speakers with force-cancelling woofers that are present in the larger model, guarantees a high level of audio quality for the consumption of media and the work that is done on projects. In addition, the screen is bright and sharp, and it supports the P3 color gamut, which ensures that color fidelity is maintained. This makes the MacBook Air 13-inch (M3) an appealing and economical solution for content creators who are looking for an alternative to the MacBook Pro.

Battery life

It never ceases to amaze me how long the battery life of Apple's silicon-powered MacBooks is, and this is one of the primary reasons why I endorse them without reservation. The MacBook Air (M3), which measures 13 inches, maintains this trend. Despite the fact that it improves performance, the M3 chip retains an impressive level of efficiency, which means that it does not significantly drain the battery.

The theoretical battery life that is given for the 15-inch MacBook Air (M3) is the same as the battery life that Apple estimates the 13-inch MacBook Air (M3) may last for up to 18 hours of Apple TV streaming and up to 15 hours of wireless internet surfing. It is possible to ascribe the parity in battery life to this efficiency, notwithstanding that the larger

15.6-inch screen of the 15-inch model requires more power than the smaller 12 inch screen.

During our battery life test, in which we constantly play a looping 1080p film until the battery runs out, the Apple MacBook Air 13-inch (M3) managed to last for 14 hours and 19 minutes. Although it is a little bit shorter than the 16 hours and 6 minutes that the M2 version was able to achieve in the same test, this is still an extremely outstanding achievement. The fact that this decline is so modest may suggest that the performance enhancements made by the M3 microprocessor have had a marginally negative effect on efficiency. In spite of this, more than 14 hours is still significant, which guarantees that you will be able to get it through an entire day of work or school on a single charge. Even during gaming, which is known to quickly deplete battery life, the MacBook Air 13-inch (M3) maintained a performance that lasted for an extended period of time.

An additional characteristic that is worth mentioning is the MacBook Air 13-inch (M3)'s ability to maintain its performance even when it is not plugged in. The performance of the MacBook Air 13-inch (M3) does not show any discernible signs of degradation in scenarios like these, in contrast to other laptops that frequently reduce their performance when using battery power in order to save the life of the battery. This, coupled with its extended battery life, renders it a favorable choice for customers in need of a portable work device. Additionally, the charger that is included is capable of replenishing the MacBook Air 13-inch (M3) in an effective manner, achieving a charge of more than fifty percent in less than an hour.

When it is not being used, the new 13-inch MacBook Air performs exceptionally well in terms of conserving battery life, just like other MacBooks. In the event that you do not use it for a number of days, you will still discover that there is a sufficient quantity of battery left when you open it. It is a credit to this efficiency that the MacBook Air 13-inch (M3) comes completely charged out of the box, allowing you to instantly begin using it after it has been set up.

CHAPTER TWO

M3 15-inch New Features

Price & availability

The Apple MacBook Air 15-inch M3 (2024) became available to customers all around the world on March 8, 2024, marking the beginning of the global launch of the product with this model.

Beginning at $1,299, £1,399, or AU$2,199, the base model comes with an M3 central processing unit (CPU) that has an 8-core CPU and a 10-core graphics processing unit (GPU), as well as 8 GB of unified memory and a 256GB solid-state drive (SSD). It is possible to configure this system to have up to 24 gigabytes of memory and a solid-state drive with a capacity of 2 terabytes. It was priced at $1,499 and had 16 gigabytes of RAM and a solid-state drive with 512 gigabytes of storage space.

The pricing of the base model of the MacBook Air 15-inch M3 remains competitive when compared to Core i7 systems such as the Dell XPS 15, despite the fact that it can be difficult to make direct comparisons between systems that use Apple silicon and those that use Intel Core i7.

Specs

The Apple MacBook Air 15-inch M3 (2024) comes in three configurations, primarily differing in memory and storage options while maintaining the same base system.

While the available configurations offer value for the price, I believe it's high time for the base model of all MacBook Airs to commence with a minimum of 512GB of storage.

Here are the specifications for each configuration:

1. MacBook Air 15-inch M3 (2024) 256GB

- Price: $1,299 / £1,399 / AU$2,199
- CPU: Apple M3 (8-core)
- Graphics: Integrated 10-core GPU
- RAM: 8GB unified memory
- Screen: 15.3-inch, 2880 x 1864 Liquid Retina display, 500 nits brightness, wide color P3 gamut
- Storage: 256GB SSD
- Ports: 2x Thunderbolt 4 (USB-C), 3.5mm headphone jack, MagSafe 3
- Wireless: Wi-Fi 6E (802.11ax), Bluetooth 5.3
- Camera: 1080p FaceTime HD webcam

- Weight: 3.3 lbs (1.51kg)
- Dimensions: 13.40 x 9.35 x 0.45 inches (340 x 212 x 15.6mm)

2. MacBook Air 15-inch M3 (2024) 512GB

- Price: $1,499 / £1,599 / AU$2,499
- CPU: Apple M3 (8-core)
- Graphics: Integrated 10-core GPU
- RAM: 8GB unified memory
- Screen: 15.3-inch, 2880 x 1864 Liquid Retina display, 500 nits brightness, wide color P3 gamut
- Storage: 512GB SSD
- Ports: 2x Thunderbolt 4 (USB-C), 3.5mm headphone jack, MagSafe 3
- Wireless: Wi-Fi 6E (802.11ax), Bluetooth 5.3
- Camera: 1080p FaceTime HD webcam
- Weight: 3.3 lbs (1.51kg)
- Dimensions: 13.40 x 9.35 x 0.45 inches (340 x 212 x 15.6mm)

3. MacBook Air 15-inch M3 (2024)

- Price: $1,699 / £1,699 / AU$2,799
- CPU: Apple M3 (8-core)
- Graphics: Integrated 10-core GPU
- RAM: 16GB unified memory
- Screen: 15.3-inch, 2880 x 1864 Liquid Retina display, 500 nits brightness, wide color P3 gamut
- Storage: 512GB SSD
- Ports: 2x Thunderbolt 4 (USB-C), 3.5mm headphone jack, MagSafe 3
- Wireless: Wi-Fi 6E (802.11ax), Bluetooth 5.3
- Camera: 1080p FaceTime HD webcam
- Weight: 3.3 lbs (1.51kg)
- Dimensions: 13.40 x 9.35 x 0.45 inches (340 x 212 x 15.6mm)

Each of these configurations can be further customized to increase memory (up to 24GB) and storage (up to 2TB).

Design

There are still some people who are dissatisfied with the fact that the MacBook Air has moved away from its original wedge-shaped design. They are curious about how this design could be adapted for a 15-inch variant. The chassis is made from recycled aluminum, and it features clean lines and corners that have been rubbed to a smooth finish.

This MacBook Air, which is equipped with M3, has proportions that are identical to those of its predecessor, the 15-inch variant. It has a width of 13.40 inches and a depth of 9.35 inches, and it has a thickness of 0.45 inches (11.5mm), which is slightly thicker than the 13-inch variant, which has a thickness of 11.3mm. Not only does it weigh 3.3 pounds, which is slightly more than half a pound heavier than its counterpart that is 13 inches, but it is still remarkably lightweight for its size. When it comes to portability, I prefer the lighter 2.7-pound MacBook Air 13-inch model, notwithstanding the fact that I appreciate the big screen.

The design of the MacBook Air 15-inch M3 is, in some respects, more streamlined than the design of the MacBook Pro. In contrast to the latter, which features fine speaker grills on either side of the keyboard, the MacBook Air 15 chooses to have a seamless metal surface throughout, despite the fact that it has extensive area for speakers. From a personal standpoint, I believe its appearance to be incredibly engaging.

When it comes to ultraportables, the Magic Keyboard from Apple continues to offer one of the most pleasurable typing experiences available. It provides a lovely tactile feedback with a sufficient amount of key travel, and the large layout enables plenty of room to operate, allowing for comfortable working conditions. Furthermore, the force touch trackpad is capacious and possesses a high level of responsiveness.

The MacBook Air 15-inch M3 does not leave users feeling overwhelmed by an excessive number of ports, as was predicted. On the other hand, it does come with a pair of Thunderbolt connections that are able to handle up to two external screens (although this is only possible while the laptop is closed).

The conveyance of data and the provision of electricity are both functions that these ports do. Effective functionality is provided by these components, which are positioned at a convenient location on one side of the laptop, adjacent to the MagSafe charge connector. In a gesture that is directed for audiophiles, the 3.5mm headphone socket may be found on the opposite side of the device. It would not be a bad idea for Apple to think about incorporating an additional USB-C connector on this side of the MacBook Air in subsequent editions of the product. Maybe they will incorporate this into their redesign plans at some point in the future.

The enormous Liquid Retina display of the 15-inch MacBook Air is one of the most notable features of this model. It provides a resolution of 2880 x 1864 pixels on its 15.3-inch screen, which is significantly higher than the resolution of 2560 x 1664 pixels that is displayed on the 13.6-inch display of the 13-inch MacBook Air. In other words, this results in hundreds of additional pixels and a huge increase in screen real estate.

Furthermore, the display is capable of supporting one billion colors and the P3 wide color gamut, both of which are amazing attributes. The visual experience is fantastic, regardless of whether you are immersing yourself in a game like Death Stranding Director's Cut or viewing a visually striking film like Spaceman on Netflix. I discovered that the screen was completely useable in a variety of lighting circumstances, despite the fact that its brightness of 500 nits might not be the maximum you could find.

One design detail that stands out is the very huge notch that is located at the very top of the screen. This notch is where the FaceTime camera is located. While participating in video chats on platforms like as Google Meets and Zoom, this 1080p camera functions quite well. One participant described the image as "crystal clear" during a one-on-one discussion, while another participant highlighted a faint cartoonish impression during a group conversation that had a more limited bandwidth. The feedback on the video quality varied.

Performance

Throughout the very short history of Apple's silicon, there has not been a single instance of disappointment. Every version goes above and beyond the one that came before it in a remarkable way. I have carefully reviewed every update, beginning with the revolutionary M1 chips and ending with the most recent M3 chips, and I have found that each and every one of them epitomizes extraordinary speed and efficiency for a System on Chip as well.

Without Apple's silicon, the 15-inch MacBook Air would most certainly continue to be a sleek and large laptop that has Apple's distinctive aesthetics. However, it would be handicapped by Intel's relatively poor desktop-class silicon.

With the addition of the M3, the 15-inch MacBook Air is transformed into a performance machine that is quick, versatile, and ready to tackle any challenge. When compared to its predecessor, the MacBook Air powered with M2 processors, its Geekbench 6 results are significantly higher.

This ultrabook performs exceptionally well in several practical applications, including as a daily driver for browsing and retrieving information, as well as a platform for demanding work such as image editing, which is backed by a wide range of onboard and cloud-based artificial intelligence operations.

The Firefly Generative AI platform was given the challenge of constructing a full scenario based on a small thumbnail of a house that was nestled in hills as part of an enthralling presentation that took place within Adobe Photoshop. The result was instantaneous and astonishingly lifelike, combining the elements of reality with a touch of ethereal allure.

Freechat, a local artificial intelligence engine, rapidly developed an outline for all of my slides when I requested that it give a presentation on horology. On the other hand, it was unable to generate the display images. It took a little bit longer for the cloud-based application to deliver a set of pictures. The images were the result of turning to Microsoft's Copilot for aid with images.

After that, I attempted to conduct the same inquiry by making use of the local artificial intelligence program known as DiffusionBee, which made it possible for me to download image models onto the MacBook. However, the quality of the photographs that were generated was noticeably lower, despite the fact that it gave results more quickly.

My abrupt talk on generative artificial intelligence in relation to a MacBook Air is something that you can thank Apple for if you are fascinated about it. In spite of the fact that they have been involved in artificial intelligence for a long time and that they have incorporated a neural engine into each and every Apple silicon system-on-chip, they have only recently started to prominently stress their AI capabilities, most likely in response to trends in the industry.

It is very clear to me that the MacBook Air 15-inch M3 will be well-equipped to take advantage of any developments in generative artificial intelligence that Apple may introduce at the World Wide Developers Conference in June of 2024.

Beyond its capabilities in artificial intelligence, the MacBook Air 15-inch M3 demonstrates that it is also a capable gaming computer. During my testing with games such as Death Stranding: Director's Cut and Asphalt 8 (while using a PlayStation Controller), the M3 displayed gameplay that was fluid and at an HD level. On the other hand, reaching the highest possible resolution in Death Stranding resulted in a notable decrease in frame rate below 30 frames per second. When playing AAA games, it is recommended to keep the resolution at a high definition level (1920x1080) in order to get a continuous frame rate of 60 percent. Even with this particular location, the amount of detail, such as the texture of Léa Seydoux's skin, continues to be outstanding.

In terms of connectivity, Apple has improved the performance of wireless networks by upgrading the WiFi from Wi-Fi 6 to Wi-Fi 6E through an upgrade. The Bluetooth protocol has not been altered from its previous version, which is version 5.3.

The operating system of a MacBook, or any other device that is part of the Apple ecosystem, is a significant factor that contributes to the appeal of purchasing one. MacOS differs from other operating systems not just because it is an advanced system but also because it gracefully transcends its age and provides a smooth user experience. Apple has successfully combined its lightning-fast and highly efficient Apple silicon with a desktop-class operating system, so ensuring a harmonious blend that does not adversely affect performance.

This cohesive system is characterized by its dependability, adaptability, and stability, and it experiences crashes only infrequently. Its attraction is further enhanced by the fact that it is compatible with the programs that you choose to use. In addition, the development of macOS and Apple Silicon is gradually establishing them as a gaming platform that is capable of competing with other platforms. Significantly, AAA games like as Lies of Pi are able to effortlessly find their footing, particularly on the spacious 15.3-inch display, which results in a gaming experience that is completely immersive.

Battery life

Let us just assume that you are curious about the reasons behind my appreciation for the most recent generation of MacBooks, it is not just their streamlined appearance and outstanding performance that I find admirable; rather, it is their fantastic battery life that actually captivates me. When it comes to personal computers, there is nothing quite like a laptop that can power through a whole workday without the need to be connected to a power source.

When it comes to their most recent models, Apple advertises 15 hours of web browsing and 18 hours of video streaming with their products. It has been demonstrated that the MacBook Air 15-inch M3 lives up to these claims, not only in our rigorous Future Labs evaluations, but also in my own personal experiences. We were able to maintain a continuous online browsing session for more than 15 hours, which is an outstanding accomplishment. The MacBook Air 15-inch M3 shown durability even when subjected to rigorous tasks such as playing Death Stranding, which is infamous for its tendency to deplete the battery faster than other games.

When compared to its smaller brother, the MacBook Air 13-inch, I had hoped that the larger MacBook Air 15-inch would offer even more substantial battery life. However, this is the only criticism I have to make.

CHAPTER THREE

Setup your new device

A thrilling experience awaits you when you purchase your brand-new Mac. This guide is designed with novices in mind, and its goal is to cover everything from the most important setup processes to the complete understanding of seamless integration. This will ensure that the beginning is both smooth and effective.

On your brand-new Mac device, we will walk you through the following important activities:

How to unbox your new MacBook Air M3 device

Unboxing a brand-new MacBook Air M3 laptop can be broken down into the following steps:

- The first step is to carefully remove the MacBook Air M3 computer from its outer packing. Make sure to keep the box in its original state so that it can be used for any future purposes.
- Examine the clean white box that contains your MacBook Air M3 for any indications of damage, making sure that it is still sealed and has not been opened throughout this process.
- It is imperative that you promptly report any problems that you find with the device's packaging or the device itself to either your supplier or directly to Apple so that they can be resolved.

- Check and recheck that you have chosen the desired amount of storage capacity for the solid-state drive (SSD) before you begin the unboxing process.

- During the process of unpacking, it is imperative that you save both the outer box and the white box that contains the Apple MacBook Air M3 for possible usage in the future.

- For the purpose of getting the MacBook Air M3 charger ready for usage, remove any protective plastic covering that may be on it.

- In order to reveal the clean appearance of the MacBook Air M3, remove all the materials that were used for packaging it.

- Make sure that your brand-new MacBook Air M3 arrives with a charge on its battery, making it ready to be powered on and properly configured.

- To ensure a safe and effective charging experience for your MacBook Air M3, make use of the 70W USB-C Power Adapter or 67W

USB-C Power Adapter that has been included.

- After the computer has been powered on, begin the process of setting up the system, being sure to swiftly update your device and install any software updates that are available by using the device Settings Panel, which can be found under **About This Mac** and **Software Updates.**

How to setup your new device

The process of setting up a new Apple MacBook Air M3 laptop can be accomplished in a number of different ways, such as by using your Apple ID, iCloud, Apple Time Machine Migration, or the Apple Migration Assistant.

Using your existing Apple ID, iCloud account, or the Apple Migration Assistant from a Time Machine backup is frequently the most frictionless way. This is especially true if you have previously used an Apple Mac computer, iPhone, or iPad.

How to setup your brand-new MacBook Air M3:

- **Use Apple iCloud:** The most effective technique involves downloading your data directly from Apple iCloud and installing any third-party software apps that may be required.

- **Apple Time Machine Backup:** Alternatively, you might deploy an Apple Time Machine backup. To begin this process, you will need to follow the instructions that appear when you power on your brand-new Mac for the first time. In the event that your Time Machine backup was produced on an earlier Mac machine, you will want a cable or converter that can convert from USB-C to USB-A.

- The use of a new USB-C external storage volume in conjunction with a USB-C to USB-A adaptor is still another alternative that might be considered. This gives you the ability to generate a backup of your current Mac machine using Time Machine, and then you may use this storage volume for your new MacBook Air M3 when you have completed the backup.

If the amount of data you need to transfer between your old and new Apple devices is minimal, the Apple Migration Assistant presents itself as a practical choice worth considering. If you want to accomplish this, you can use the Wi-Fi network at your house or place of business.

How to copy data from an existing Apple Mac device to your new device

You can transfer data from your previous Apple Mac computer to your new one using a number of different methods, including the following:

- **Apple iCloud:** Using Apple iCloud, you may synchronize your data across all of your devices in a seamless manner. When it comes to transferring different kinds of information, such as documents, photographs, and other types of files, this method is very convenient.

- **Time Machine Backup**: If you have a Time Machine backup of your previous Mac, you will be able to effortlessly restore your data onto your new Mac. In this way, you can rest assured that all of your data, settings, and programs will be transferred smoothly.

- **Mac to Mac via Apple Migration Assistant: By** enabling you to immediately move data from your old Mac to your new Mac over a network or by using a Thunderbolt or FireWire cable, Apple Migration Assistant is a built-in utility that streamlines the process of transferring data from one Mac to another.

- **External Storage:** If you only need to transfer a few files or folders, using an external storage volume, such as a USB flash drive or an external hard drive, is a straightforward solution that you can consider.

- **Cloud Storage Services**: Cloud storage services include services such as Microsoft OneDrive and Dropbox, which provide cloud storage solutions that allow you to transfer and view your files from any location. This comes in especially handy for documents and files that are on the smaller side.

- **Memory Stick:** Using a memory stick is a straightforward and portable method of transferring data between your old Mac and your new Mac, provided that you are only moving a small number of documents between the two computers.

You also have the option of signing into your Apple ID account, which will instantly sync your iCloud data and settings to your new Mac. This will make the process of setting up your newly acquired Mac more simplified.

More specifically, while using iCloud:

- It is possible to upload files and documents to iCloud by dragging and dropping them onto the iCloud icon in Mac Air M3 Finder. This is the case if you simply have a few files and documents. If you want to access these files on your brand-new MacBook Air M3, you will need to disable the Desktop and Documents option and then pick iCloud.

- Let's assume that your new MacBook Air M3 has a restricted amount of storage space, you have the option to opt out of downloading particular items from iCloud. These items include Apple TV and Apple Photos. In addition, you have the option of establishing a separate Apple Photos System Library or managing the libraries that you already possess. Prior to making any modifications, you should think about calling Apple Photos Support in order to receive expert guidance on how to manage your Apple Photos collection.

How to use Apple iCloud to setup your MacBook Air M3

Assuming that you initially made use of a macOS High Sierra or a later edition on your existing Apple Mac computer and your data is stored on Apple iCloud, the method of transferring it to your new Apple MacBook Air M3 is a basic one.

- To move your data from your previous Mac to your new MacBook Air M3, all you need to do is log in to your iCloud account using your Apple ID.

How to use Apple Time machine to set up your device

Due to the fact that the Apple MacBook Air M3 is equipped with USB-C ports, it is necessary to make use of a USB-A to USB-C converter in order to make use of the Apple Migration Assistant in order to transfer data from an Apple Time Machine Backup to an Apple MacBook Air M3 laptop.

- It is possible that you will need a USB-C to USB-A adapter or cable in order to connect your Apple Time Machine backup storage volume to your new MacBook Air M3 if the backup storage volume uses a USB-A port connection. This is the case if you have created an Apple Time Machine backup for your previous or older Apple Mac computer and have a significant amount of data that you wish to migrate.

- The most advantageous and effective technique is to choose to transfer data from your existing Apple Mac computer to your new MacBook Air M3 while you are engaged in the process of setting up the new MacBook Air M3 on the setup screen of the new device.

- When transferring data with Apple Time Machine, you have the ability to choose which user accounts, data, and apps to move. This gives you a great deal of flexibility.

- The backup created by Apple Time Machine will automatically decide which applications should be copied. Examples of software that are generally pre-installed on new Apple Mac computers include Apple Safari, Apple Mail, Apple Calendars, Apple Contacts, Photos for Mac, Apple Preview, and Apple's office suite, which includes Pages, Numbers, and Keynote. These applications can be downloaded for free from the Apple App Store.

- You are still able to transfer data from your Apple Time Machine backup storage volume to your new Apple Mac computer, even if you have already finished the process of setting up your Apple Mac computer.

- In the case that you are using the Apple Migration Assistant and come across an error message that indicates there is not enough storage available, it is recommended that you seek the aid of a professional in order to remedy the issue.

How to use Apple migration assistant to transfer data from Mac to Mac

You are able to transfer your data without any interruptions by making use of the Apple Migration Assistant tool, which is already installed on your brand-new Apple MacBook Air M3 prior to your purchase. Depending on whether you have chosen the Apple Mac computer with the Ethernet port option or not, you have the choice of accomplishing this task using a Wi-Fi wireless network connection or through an Ethernet connection.

If you want to transfer data from OneDrive or Dropbox to your new Apple Mac, all you need to do is install the client software for the corresponding service, such as Microsoft OneDrive or Dropbox.

Alternatively, a USB memory stick that is equipped with a USB C to USB A adaptor can be used for the transfer of lesser amounts of data in situations where iCloud, OneDrive, or Dropbox are not involved.

Additionally, it is important to note that dual USB A and USB C memory sticks are now available. This makes it possible to transfer data quickly between computers that are equipped with USB A ports and the new Mac Air M3 computer, which is compatible with USB C devices.

CHAPTER FOUR

Additional steps on setting up your device

How to set up internet

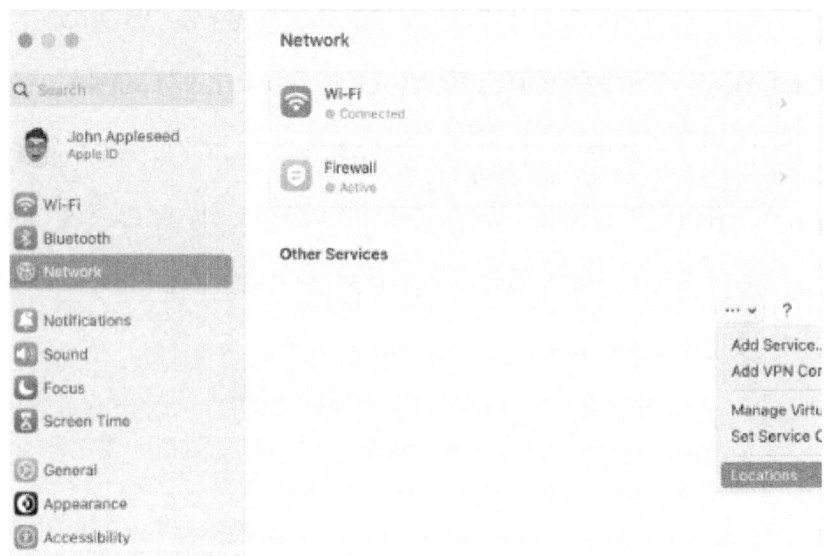

In order to get started with this new Mac device, let's begin by ensuring that your internet connection is operational. In the event that you are accessing the internet with an Ethernet cable, you need only plug it into the rear of your Mac as you normally would.

Follow these steps in order to establish a connection to a Wi-Fi network:

- Tap the **Apple emblem** located in the upper-left corner of the screen, and then select "System Preferences."
- Select "Wi-Fi" from the list of available options, and check to see that it is turned on.
- To access your Wi-Fi network, locate it and select it from the selection that drops down. You will be required to enter your password, and after that, you will have to wait a few seconds for the connection to create itself.

How to Change scroll direction

It is possible that you will observe, during your initial training on the Mac, that the default orientation of scrolling may be different from what you are used to. Adapting this setting requires you to follow these steps:

- First and foremost, access the **System Preferences menu** by clicking on the Apple icon.
- Also, access **Pointer control** by navigating to Accessibility.
- Make adjustments to the Mouse and Trackpad Options inside this menu to suit your preferences regarding the direction of scrolling and the speed of clicking.

Visual customization

It should come as no surprise that your new device provides a wide range of customization choices, allowing you to personalize its design to your preference. Through the System Settings, you have the ability to easily modify the desktop backdrop, the screensaver, and the color elements included in the desktop.

Altering your login image to something that is unique and fashionable is another option for adding a touch of personalization to your account. You can visually personalize your new device by following the steps outlined in for new Mac users, which begin with:

- Accessing the **System Preferences** menu by clicking on the Apple icon.
- Select the **Appearance option** to gain access to the customization panel, which allows you to adjust a variety of desktop characteristics in accordance with your personalized preferences.

How to set up your printer

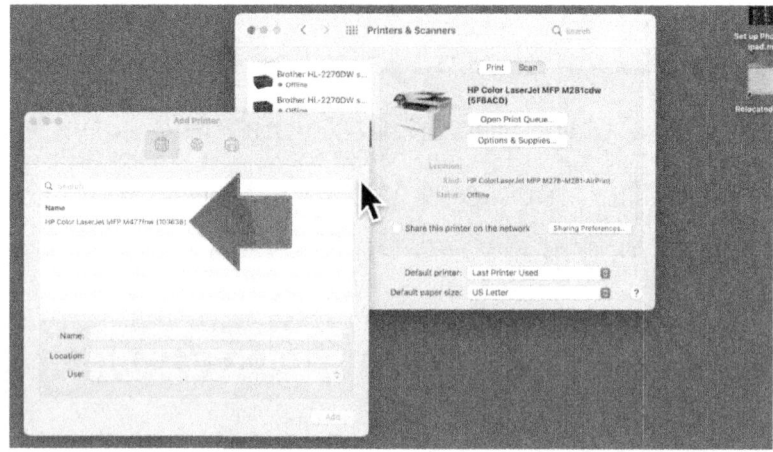

The process of installing printers on a Mac is often simple, even for those who are just starting out. This is especially true when the printer in question is already connected to the network. What follows is a condensed version of the instructions for connecting your printer to your Mac laptop:

- Start by selecting **System Preferences** from the menu that appears after clicking on the Apple icon.
- Head over to the **Printers & Scanners section.**
- The search for accessible printers will be carried out automatically by your system. To

manually include your printer, you can manually include it by clicking the Add Printers, Scanners, or Fax option if it is not identified or listed otherwise.

There is a possibility that you will be required to install additional software when connecting by USB; nonetheless, the process should be uncomplicated.

How to get your backups ready

Through the use of Time Machine, Apple streamlines the process of integrating backup capability into Mac Air M3 device. For those who are just starting out with their MacBook, this software is a godsend because it offers an automated method of backing up important files and programs and simplifies the process of recovering data in the event of any accidents.

It is possible to set up Time Machine to create backups of your Mac automatically, which will ensure that your information and applications may be restored in the same condition as they were in the past.

It is possible to configure your backups using Time Machine in the following manner:

- You can access the **System Preferences** by either clicking on the Apple icon or searching for it in Spotlight.
- Proceed to General > Time Machine on your browser.
- Also, select your backup destination, then click "Set Up Disk," after which you should click "Add Backup Disk."

How to add users

Establishing additional user accounts is a prudent course of action to take if you believe that your new Mac will be used by a number of different people. This makes it possible for everyone to customize their experience by using a variety of different applications and configurations.

Follow these straightforward steps in order to add users:

- You can access **System Preferences** by clicking the Apple Icon or by looking at the Dock on your computer.
- Click the "Add User" button after selecting "Users & Groups" from the drop-down menu.
- To add new users to your Mac laptop, you will need to verify that you are an administrator.

How to Install cybersecurity

It was typical practice in the past to use a Mac without antivirus software, but in today's world, doing so is not recommended. There has been a notable rise in the amount of malicious software that targets mac devices, including ransomware for example.

Because of this, it is absolutely necessary to give some thought to installing an application such as MacKeeper when you first start using a MacBook. In addition to its other advantages, our built-in antivirus software offers protection in real time and scans whenever they are needed.

If you want to protect your MacBook with MacKeeper's Antivirus, you should:

- Launch the **MacKeeper application**.
- Proceed to the Antivirus features located in the panel on the left side of the screen.
- Real-time protection should be activated, and full disk access should be granted.
- A scan can be started by selecting the **Start Scan button**, and if any risks are found, you can choose to move them to the quarantine area.

CHAPTER FIVE

Finding your way around your new

Device

MacBook Air M3 exhibits several similarities to Windows in terms of its navigational capabilities. Window-based visual interfaces are used by both programs, and they are browsed through the use of a combination of mouse and keyboard inputs.

In both operating systems, it is normal practice to perform fundamental activities like as right-clicking to open files, dragging and dropping items into folders, and using a trash can to dispose of files that have been recently deleted.

However, there are also considerable disparities between the two. In order to assist novices in becoming acquainted with the operating system, this chapter will focus on highlighting important aspects of your new device.

The Dock

The device Dock is located at the bottom of your screen and serves as a collection of essential shortcuts to applications that are installed on your Apple laptop. This includes both the apps that come pre-installed on your Macintosh as well as those that you have personally added. You have the ability to personalize your Dock by clicking and dragging app icons, allowing you to adjust it to your needs and tastes.

It is as simple as dragging shortcuts from the Dock; rest assured that this operation does not result in the uninstallation of the applications that are associated with the shortcuts. In addition, you may access additional options that are associated with the applications that are located in your Dock by simply right-clicking on the Dock.

Spotlight

Specifically, the search feature that is included in your Mac device is referred to as Spotlight. Besides searching through your Mac for goods, Spotlight also searches the internet, the App Store, and a variety of other sources in addition to searching via your Mac. When you use a Mac, this multifunctional feature will prove to be extremely useful for completing routine activities and will increase your productivity.

Clicking on the icon that looks like a magnifying glass and is placed in the upper right-hand corner of your screen or pressing the Cmd key and the space bar will bring up Spotlight. Simply enter your query into the search window of Spotlight, and it will immediately present you with recommendations that will be of assistance to you.

Menu Bar

At the very top of the screen on your MacBook, you will find the menu bar, which was developed to improve the overall user experience. The contents of it are dynamically modified in accordance with the program that you are currently using. In the event that you are browsing with Safari, for instance, you will be presented with options and settings that are exclusive to Safari.

The recognizable Apple logo, which is always present regardless of the application that is being used, can be found at the very left side of the screen. Using this logo, you can quickly access shortcuts and functions that are available across the entire system, such as restarting, shutting down, or logging out. The navigation is simplified as a result of this uniformity, particularly for individuals who are new to Mac systems.

The notification area is located on the right side of the menu bar. It contains crucial shortcuts to a variety of programs and settings, such as Wi-Fi, date, and time, which ensures that commonly used services can be accessed quickly.

The App Store

Macintosh computers, much like iPhones, come equipped with their very own App Store. On the other hand, in contrast to iOS, MacBook Air M3 gives users the ability to independently download and install applications from sources other than the App Store.

The utilization of the App Store offers an additional layer of protection, despite the fact that this versatility is useful. Apple takes great care in selecting its material, thereby protecting its customers from potentially hazardous applications that may include malware infections.

In the App Store, you will find a wealth of applications that were built by Apple. Each of these applications is designed to ensure that your MacBook operates in a secure and flawless manner.

However, it is essential to exercise caution while downloading applications from third-party sources wherever possible. In order to guarantee the security and dependability of your Mac experience from the very beginning, it is recommended that you read evaluations that are available online.

Activity Monitor

A similar application known as the Activity Monitor is available for use on MacBook Air M3 device, just like the Task Manager that is included with Windows. Making use of the Spotlight or going to Applications > Utilities are both viable options for gaining access to it. Initially, the data may appear to be difficult to understand and intimidating; yet, it offers insights into the consumption of your MacBook memory, central processing unit (CPU), energy, disk, and network.

The Activity Monitor gives you the ability to control processes and terminate them if necessary, which is extremely helpful when debugging program issues or getting acquainted with mac. This is true regardless of whether you are a rookie or an expert user of a Mac.

Safari

It is highly recommended that individuals who are new to using a Mac become familiar with Safari, which is a web browser that is specifically designed for Macs. Safari is supported by a large number of people within the Macintosh development community and provides a comprehensive collection of plugins.

It is favored by a large number of users and possesses features that are common in contemporary browsers, such as a mode that allows for private browsing. On the other hand, it is important to note that you are not restricted to using Safari; popular alternatives such as Chrome are also available for your new device, which ensures that you have more options for your browsing experience.

Ask Siri

Siri is Apple's voice assistant, and it is actually the same voice assistant that is built into iPhones. It makes it easier to perform a variety of tasks, such as launching applications and completing online searches.

- To activate Siri on your Mac, you may either press and hold the Command and Space keys simultaneously or click the Siri icon that is found in the upper right corner of your menu bar.
- By incorporating Siri into your Mac, you may ease general chores on your laptop and streamline search operations.

Apps

The fact that novice users of a MacBook do not first become familiar with the operation of Mac applications is a possible obstacle for them. Applications in your MacBook Air M3 are arranged in a logical fashion within the Applications folder, which may be accessed with the Finder application.

Most of the time, this directory does not have any more subfolders, in contrast to Windows. This simplicity is a result of the fact that applications on your new device are self-contained, with each application being represented by a single icon that can be launched by double-clicking.

The core application itself continues to be self-contained, despite the fact that certain applications can require other files that are stored in other locations on your Mac in order to function. On the other hand, when such applications are removed, leftover files can be left behind, which would require further administration.

System Preferences

For Mac users, this is comparable to the Control Panel that is seen in Windows. Managing the operation of your Mac and modifying the settings of the system are both handled through this central location.

- Simply clicking on the Apple icon that is located in the menu bar is one of the most common ways to access the System Preferences. Accessing System Preferences is easily accessible.
- When you arrive at that location, you will discover a wealth of options that you may customize to suit your preferences. These options include screen settings, Bluetooth connections, network configurations, and printer configurations.

Getting familiar with these options can significantly improve your experience with your Mac; nonetheless, it is important to exercise caution when making changes in order to avoid unforeseen repercussions.

CHAPTER SIX

Split View Feature

There is a good chance that you have at least ten tabs open at any given moment, if you are anything like me. When you are working from home on a desktop or laptop, it can be very annoying and time-consuming to scroll through each tab in order to find the one that you require.

You may improve the efficiency of your productivity by adopting split-screen mode, which enables you to keep two windows open at the same time. This eliminates the need to scan through tabs, which leads to inefficiency. The split-screen mode is quite useful for a variety of tasks, including the analysis of data for a report, the maintenance of chat windows while concentrating on other activities, and even the enjoyment of a video while simultaneously performing other jobs.

Your good fortune lies in the fact that MacBook Air M3 come equipped with a function known as split-screen mode, which allows you to arrange two applications or independent browser windows side by side on your display. Without the necessity for frequent mouse navigation or the usage of shortcuts such as Command + Tab, this functionality makes it possible to navigate between windows in a simple manner.

The following is an in-depth guide that will walk you through the process of configuring and navigating split-screen mode on your new Mac device.

How to enter Split View on your new Mac device

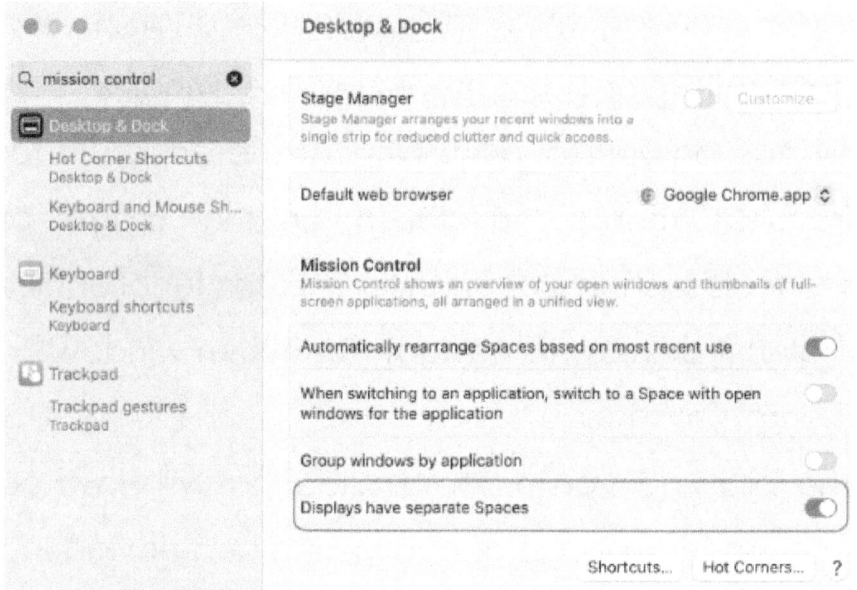

- You need to make sure that none of the windows you want to use is configured to use the entire screen.

- It is recommended that you position your cursor over the green button that is situated in the upper left corner of one of the windows that you intend to use. It is recommended that you linger over the window until a drop-down option appears rather than clicking on it immediately in order to maximize it.

- The drop-down box allows you to select either "Tile Window to Left of Screen" or "Tile Window to Right of Screen" as your preferred option. After that, the split-screen option will be automatically activated on your Mac.

- It will appear on the opposite side of the screen that the windows that are still open are displayed. Choose the window that you want to take up the other half of the screen, and it will fill the area that is left over after you make your selection.

- Make use of the slider that is situated in the middle of the screen in order to make adjustments to the size of the windows.

- If you have Split View enabled, you will be able to view both windows concurrently without any interruptions, which will allow you to multitask more effectively.

How to exit split screen

It is possible to exit the split-screen layout in the following manner once you have completed it:

- Move your pointer to the top of the screen and wait for the buttons to adjust the size of each window to appear in the upper left corner of the window.

- The current window can be closed by clicking the red button, and the split-screen mode can be exited by clicking the green button.

- Be not concerned! If you are using full-screen mode, your other window will remain open; it will simply be hidden. Pressing the **Mission Control button (F3)** located on the top row of your keyboard will allow you to obtain access to it once more.

- Both the Desktop and the window that you had in split-screen mode will be displayed at the very top of the screen for you to choose from. If you want to exit the full-screen mode, click the other window, and then use the green sizing button that is located in the top left corner of the window.

For those of you who, like me, frequently require more than two windows open at the same time, you have the ability to manually resize windows so that they can fit three or four windows on your screen at the same time. It is important to keep in mind, however, that making use of tiled windows will result in a more visually appealing experience.

The keyboard shortcut for split screen

One of the many useful options that can be accessed by keyboard shortcuts on a MacBook Air M3 is the ability to run the app in split-screen mode.

- The first step is to enter full-screen mode by pressing Control, Command, and F simultaneously. You can then reach Mission Control by pressing the F3 key on your keyboard.
- Once you are there, you can easily drag and drop the second application that you want to

include on your split screen next to the window that appears initially.

- Immediately following the appearance of the "+" symbol, a preview of the split screen arrangement will be displayed. Once you have returned to the apps that have been tiled, you will find that you are in Split View.

You have the ability to personalize your own keyboard shortcut, which will let you access Split View even more quickly. Open the System Preferences menu, then select Keyboard, then Keyboard Shortcuts, and finally select App Shortcuts. It is possible to add a command with the name "**Tile Window to Left of Screen**" by clicking the "+" symbol and selecting the shortcut that you desire.

Your active window will tile to the left side of the screen after it has been launched, which will allow you to select a second window for incorporation into your split screen arrangement in a seamless manner.

Reasons why your Mac M3 won't do Split screen

- In the first place, check to see that you are not now operating in fullscreen mode. The split screen feature is only functional when the window is in its usual view.

- In the event that fullscreen mode is not the problem, go to the **System Preferences menu** and select **Desktop & Dock**. Make sure that "Displays have separate Spaces" is enabled by scrolling down to the bottom of the page. If it is not already enabled, activate it.

- It is recommended that you check that your new Mac device is updated to the latest version if you are unable to locate the option in the **Mission Control menu.** Simply click the **Apple icon** located in the upper left menu, and then select **About this Mac** to determine the current version of your operating system. You can update to a newer version by clicking the **Software Update button** that is located on the screen you are currently using.

- Take into consideration that not all applications allow split screens. It is highly likely that the application does not have this capability if you have attempted all the procedures listed above and it still does not tile in split-screen mode.

The official "Split View" function on a Mac instantly splits two windows into full screen mode. This allows you to split screens without having to go to full screen mode. On the other hand, if you would rather not use full-screen view (maybe because you want to switch between browser tabs in a rapid manner), you have the ability to manually resize and position your windows so that they fit into the space that you require. When compared to Split View, this method provides a greater degree of customization, enabling you to personalize the screen layout to suit your exact preferences.

CHAPTER SEVEN

How to use the Spotlight and screenshot feature

Tips and tricks on how to use this feature

It doesn't matter if you're only looking for files or have a better understanding of how to navigate the system; Spotlight search is an extremely useful feature for any Mac user. Through familiarizing yourself with these strategies, you will be able to manage your Mac M3 device in an effective manner without having to rely on the mouse.

1. **Make use of the shortcut on your keyboard for Spotlight.**

As an alternative to clicking the magnifying glass icon located in the upper-right corner, you can use the keyboard shortcut Command-spacebar to accomplish the same task more quickly.

2. Make adjustments to the size and position of Spotlight.

If your search produces a large number of results, you can modify the Spotlight window by sliding its bottom edge to enlarge it or by moving its top edge to move it. Your device will remember the most recent position and size settings, which will ensure that subsequent searches are consistent with the previous ones. Simply clicking and holding the magnifying glass symbol will allow you to return Spotlight to its original set of settings.

3. Embrace natural language queries

You can currently use Spotlight to conduct queries using natural language phrases. Spotlight can be instructed to display "photos from yesterday" or "files from last month" in order to facilitate the speedy search for particular objects.

4. Sports and Weather

Spotlight allows you to rapidly see your current conditions as well as a 10-day prediction without requiring you to leave the app. Simply type "weather" into Spotlight. For the forecast for the City by the Bay or any other city of your choosing, enter "weather in San Francisco" in the search bar. It is also possible to obtain sports scores (for example, "Red Sox score") and schedules (for example, "Ohio State schedule") directly within Spotlight in the same manner.

5. Instant Calculations

While the calculator software that comes pre-installed on your Mac device is a good option for performing quick calculations, you can also rely on Spotlight.

6. Currency Conversion

Spotlight is able to give you with up-to-date exchange rates, so that you may use it whether you are traveling internationally or keeping a watch on the worldwide currency markets.

7. Open Finder

To open a file that you have found by searching for it, highlight it in Spotlight and then press the Enter key. Instead, you can open the folder in Finder that contains the file by pressing the Command-Enter simultaneously.

8. Track down a file

While highlighting a file in Spotlight, you can expose the location of the file by holding down the Command key. Within the Spotlight application, the path will be displayed along the bottom border of the right panel.

9. Look through the search results.

Spotlight organizes the results of a search into a number of distinct sections, including Top Hits, Documents, Spreadsheets, Wikipedia, Suggested Websites, and Definitions. Combining the up and down arrow keys with the Command key will allow you to skip between parts.

10.   Access Definitions Quickly

Simply pressing the Command-L key will immediately take you to the definition of the term you are searching for.

11.   Switch to Google

If you would rather conduct a specific search using Google rather than Spotlight, you can easily start a new tab in your default browser by using the Command-B key. This will allow you to use your default search engine.

12.   Clear Search Bar Effortlessly

In order to quickly clear the search field in Spotlight, press the Escape key (or the Command-Delete key). Repeat the press of the Escape key to close Spotlight. You also have the option of clicking outside of Spotlight in order to disable it.

Different shortcuts on how to take a

screenshot

Screenshots make it possible to more easily manage tasks such as producing duplicates of travel or sports tickets, capturing receipts for digital transactions, and capturing receipts for digital purchases. This process is made easier on a MacBook Air M3 by a number of shortcuts, including:

- **Entire Screen Capture:** In order to quickly capture your entire screen, press the Command key, followed by the Shift key, and then the number 3. When it comes to fast taking screenshots of videos without missing any frames, this method is really helpful.
- **Selective Area Capture:** The command, shift, and four shortcuts change your mouse pointer into a crosshair, which enables you to choose and drag the frame in order to capture a certain portion of your screen or an

application window. This capture technique is known as selective area capture.

- **Window or Element Capture:** To capture a particular window, application, or element, press Command + Shift + 4 plus the space bar. This will allow you to capture the window or element in question. By performing this operation, your mouse cursor will be transformed into a camera icon, which will enable you to select the element that you want to use. There will be a light blue filter that will highlight a target element while you are hovering over it. This will indicate that the element has been selected. The results of using this strategy are screenshots that appear more organized and have a minor shadow effect.

How to easily take a screen recording

Sometimes, individuals are able to comprehend topics more efficiently through the use of visual mediums such as videos as opposed to instructions that are written down. When faced with situations like this, it is more beneficial to opt for a screen recording rather than making extensive lists.

- When you want to start recording your screen, you must first press Command, Shift, and 5.
- Following that, you should move your cursor to the toolbar that is located close to the bottom of your screen.
- You will see that there are two icons that are highlighted: one on the right with a dashed border, which allows you to specify a specific region for recording, and the other on the left, which captures your full screen.
- After selecting the option that best suits your needs, click the "Record" button.
- The recording can be terminated by either selecting **the Stop symbol** that is situated in the Menu bar at the top of the screen or by pressing the Command, Control, and Esc keys simultaneously.

How to save screenshots and recordings

Taking screenshots and recording audio are both stored to your desktop by default, which can rapidly cause your workspace to get cluttered. On the other hand, you have the ability to choose a separate location for saving these files, which enables you to keep your desktop organized. In this manner:

- Press Command, Shift, and 5.
- To access the options, click on "Options."
- Select "Other Location" from the drop-down menu that appears under "Save to," or select one of the pre-selected destinations, such as Documents or Messages, to save your screenshots and recordings in a specific folder of your choosing.

Easily Preview Files

You are able to see the contents of multiple files in Finder or on your Desktop that have titles or appearances that are similar to one another. This allows you to avoid opening all of the files. To access a file, you need to click on it once and then press the spacebar. It is possible to view the file without any need to start the Preview application. After pressing the spacebar once more, the preview will be closed.

You can also choose a file, hold down the spacebar to preview it, and then release the spacebar to quit the preview mode. This will allow you to view and exit the file in a short amount of time.

While you are previewing files, copy the text:

It is possible to extract text from a document or snapshot while previewing the file. This is something that you can do if you need to. Simply picking the file and using the spacebar will allow you to preview it. Once you have done that, move your mouse pointer over the text you want to modify, and the cursor icon will appear on your screen. As is customary, you are now able to pick and copy text.

You can convert screenshots that contain a lot of text, such recipes, into documents for better organization with the help of this function, which is especially helpful for screenshots that contain many words.

CHAPTER EIGHT

How to take a Photo

While taking a picture with your iPhone is now easier than it has ever been, have you ever given any thought to how you would go about taking a picture with your Mac computers? It is possible that you will find yourself in a situation where you require the use of the built-in camera on your Mac.

This could be for the purpose of updating a profile photograph during the registration process or capturing a moment during a video conference. Your command is waiting for the camera, which is positioned in a handy location in the middle of the screen on your Mac.

The purpose of this chapter is to illustrate how to make the most of the capabilities of the built-in webcam that comes with your new device in order to easily take photos.

How to open Mac webcam

There are some people who are not familiar with how to use the webcam interface, despite the fact that Mac users may simply identify it on their screens. Taking pictures with the webcam on a MacBook Air M3 can be accomplished in a number of different ways, including the utilization of third-party software or the application that is integrated into the Mac operating system called Photo Booth. Make sure you follow these instructions in order to access Photo Booth on your Mac:

- In the Mac Dock, choose **the Finder icon** by clicking on it.
- Proceed to the **Applications section** located in the left column. Once you have done that, locate the Photo Booth by scrolling down in the right window.

- Photo Booth may also be accessed using **Launchpad** or by searching for it using Mac Spotlight. Both of these options are available to you.
- You may open the software by either double-clicking it or right-clicking and selecting "Open."

How to take a photo on Mac with camera

The bottom of the Photo Booth window is divided into three pieces, which you will notice when you access the window. With the help of these parts, you will be able to take a picture, record a video, and apply a variety of engaging effects to the pictures you have on your Mac. How to take a picture with a photo booth is explained in great depth in the following:

- The first step is to start up Photo Booth on your device. Following the activation of the webcam on the Mac, which will be signaled by a green light directly next to it, you will immediately be able to see yourself displayed on the screen.

- In the second step, you will click on the "Effects" button in order to investigate the wide variety of effects that Photo Booth provides. You may find out which filter you like most by trying out a variety of filters, such as Space Alien, Dizzy, Frog, and others.

- For the third step, you have the option of taking a single photo or numerous photos in rapid succession, depending on your personal preference. Step one is to navigate to the buttons located in the bottom left corner of the screen. The first icon allows for the capture of multiple photos in a row, while the second icon starts a single capture.

- Click on the **red button** in the middle of the screen to take a picture on your Mac when you have finished adjusting the settings and selecting the effects you want to use. Following the beginning of the countdown, which will last for three seconds, your photograph will be taken.

How to save and find photos on Mac

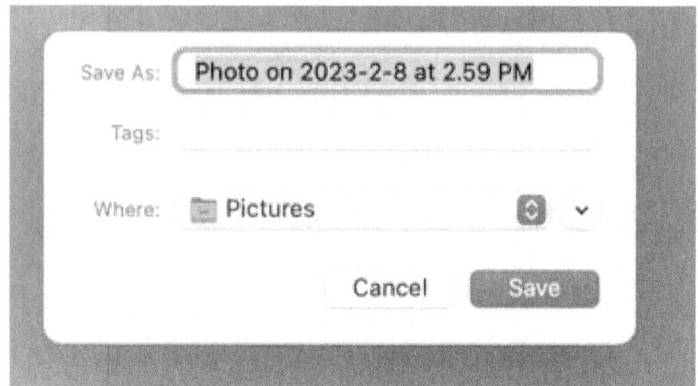

Whenever you take a picture on your MacBook Air M3 device, it will show up in the lower-right hand corner of the screen where the program is shown. In order to preserve and locate your photographs, please follow the procedures below:

- To begin, right-click on the photograph that you have taken. Choose "Export" from the list of available options. If you want to get rid of images that aren't to your liking, you should opt to click the "Delete" button instead.

- In the second step, you will need to give your photo a name and a tag within the export box. If you want to save it, select a location to save it to, such as "Pictures" or "Desktop." Finally, to confirm, click the "Save" button.

- To continue taking images on your Mac, simply click the "X" button that is located on the particular shot that you are currently taking.

How to take a photo on Mac with right-click menu

Let us assume that you frequently need to snap photographs on your new Mac device, there is a more straightforward approach to launching the Photo Booth program. This approach eliminates the need to navigate through directories and applications each time. Streamlining the process of shooting photos on a Mac can be accomplished with the assistance of a convenient program such as iBoysoft MagicMenu, which allows you to activate Photo Booth with only one click.

The right-click enhancer for Mac that stands out as the best is iBoysoft MagicMenu. It gives you the power to personalize the menu that appears in the Finder and dramatically boosts your productivity. Among the many services that it offers, the "Launch With" category is particularly important because it speeds up the process of gaining access to important applications such as Terminal and Visual Studio Code. Through the process of manually adding Photo Booth to this category, you will be able to effortlessly summon it with a right-click on your Mac desktop, which will ease the process of capturing images on a Mac.

In addition to the "Launch With" functionality, iBoysoft MagicMenu offers a wide range of additional helpful capabilities, like "Copy To," "Move To," "Quick Access," and a great deal more. These functionalities are all meant to enhance the usefulness of your right-click menu. Downloading this strong right-click extender for free and giving it a try now will allow you to experience the ease that it offers.

FAQs about how to take a photo on Mac

1. What is the general method how to capture a picture on all Mac Air devices:

- To launch Mac Spotlight, press the Command key + S at the same time. You can choose "Photo Booth" from the list of results after typing it into the search bar.
- You can personalize your image by adding the graphic effects you want. Click the camera icon on your MacBook Air when you are ready to take the picture in order to capture it.
- Once the image has been captured, right-click on it and select "Save" to save it to the location of your choosing.

CHAPTER NINE

How to find photos

The trip that is life is braided with memories, and perhaps there is no better way to preserve those memories than by taking pictures of them with our mobile phones or digital cameras? The majority of the time, we save these priceless moments on our mobile devices, such as our iPhones or MacBooks. Once in a while, we have the desire to remember by looking through old photographs of our loved ones, our cherished pets, or our most memorable holidays.

Nevertheless, it can be difficult to find these memories amidst the clutter that we have created with our digital devices. The purpose of this chapter is to make the process of locating your images on a MacBook as easy and quick as possible. How about we dive in together and find out what the steps are?

How to find your photos on Mac

The following are basic steps on how you can locate or find photos on your new device;

- Make use of **the Dock** to access the Photos application on your Mac, which will allow you to quickly locate your photographs. When you have found it, double-click on it to open it.
- As soon as you access your photo library, it will be shown in chronological order, beginning with the most recent photographs. However, you also have the option of organizing your photographs into a variety of categories, which can be accessed through the left panel.
- Only a small fraction of the valuable content that is stored on your device is comprised of your photo collection. In order to protect your

data, you should establish passwords to the files and folders that you have on your Mac.

- Memories, People, and Places are some of the categories that are easily accessible within the Photos app, which allows for quick categorization. If you want to access the contents of a particular category, you need only select it from the list.

- Despite the fact that the default view displays all the photos, you have the ability to narrow your search by applying filters. In order to locate older photographs in a timely manner, select the desired filter option from the list of options located at the top of the window. You can select from Years, Months, or Dates.

How to find imported photos on Mac

When you look at the side panel of the Photos app, you will see that there is a category labeled "Imports" that is located in the lower half of the Photos area. It is quite convenient that all the photographs that you have brought in from your phone or other devices are stored in here section.

You will find your imported photographs nicely organized by date if you navigate to photographs > Imports and then look for them. Imports will present you with a list of your most recent imports as soon as you access the section. A straightforward scroll upwards is all that is required to gain access to prior imports.

You have the ability to filter the imported photographs based on categories, which you can do for a more specific search. The "Showing: All Items" button can be found in the upper-right hand corner of the Imports window. After clicking on it, you will be able to choose from a variety of options, including Favorites, Edited, Photos, or Videos. Because of this, you will be able to zero in on particular categories of foreign content that you have imported.

How to find downloaded photos on Mac

When you save ideas from Pinterest and download them for later use, you frequently find that they are helpful. Accessing these images that you have saved on your Mac is a simple process. To access the Downloads menu, simply navigate to the Finder in the taskbar of your Mac and pick it from the left panel.

Locate the photographs you want to download by scrolling through your downloads catalog. Make use of the grouping icon, which can be found in the top-right corner of the screen, near to the upload symbol. This will allow you to access the grouping icon more quickly. After the option has been chosen, select "Kind" from the selection that drops down.

At this point, your downloads will be organized according to the categories that they belong to. Your photographs should be located within the "Images" category, which you should look for. This method is especially helpful when dealing with a large number of downloads because it provides a more streamlined approach to locating your photographs.

How to restore deleted photos on Mac

We frequently find ourselves shooting a large number of photographs, which can occasionally lead to the deletion of photos without our knowledge while we are cleaning up our Mac. It is fortunate that there is a way to rescue your prized photographs in the event that such a mishap takes place, as Macs keep deleted photographs for a period of up to forty days.

- Launch the **Photos app** and navigate to the tab labeled "Recently Deleted" in the left panel. This is the last option available under the Photos section. This will allow you to access the photos that you have deleted.

- You have the ability to restore your deleted images here, which will prevent any irreversible loss. Keep an eye on the amount of time that is left until your Mac deletes them permanently, which is displayed below each photo based on the date that it was deleted.

- In the event that you have four days left to retrieve a photo, for instance, you will see the phrase "4 days left" beneath the photo. A photo that has been deleted can be recovered by selecting it once and then clicking on the **Recover button**, which is placed in the upper-right hand corner of the window. Your photo will be restored to your Library.

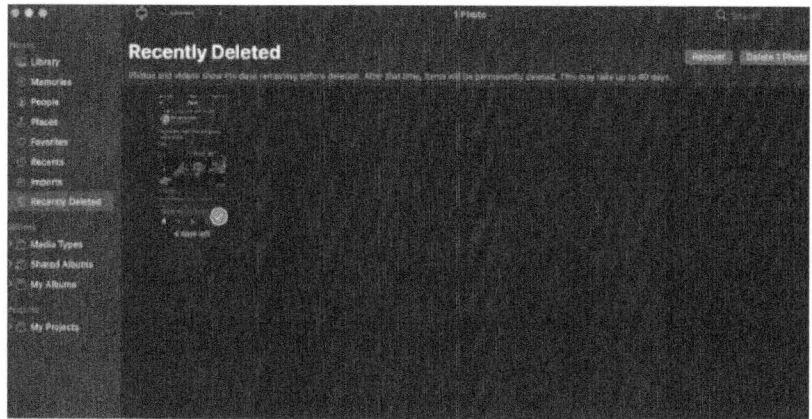

Why you should store your photos on your iCloud

Your photographs are treasured recollections that are intended to endure a lifetime. It is highly recommended that you choose to manage them using your iCloud account on your Mac M3 device in order to preserve their longevity and accessibility. To explain why:

- **Maintains the picture's quality**

The high-resolution quality of your photographs is preserved when you store them on iCloud, which guarantees that they will look their best whether they are printed or shared.

- **Help with a Wide Range of Files**

Apple's iCloud service allows users to save a wide variety of file types, including JPEG, PNG, and even raw photos. The ability to manage, edit, and share your images across all of your Apple devices is effortless, and any changes you make will be synchronized immediately.

- **Stronger Safety Measures**

You add an additional layer of safety to your images by backing them up to iCloud, which is in addition to being stored locally. CloudKit is a framework developed by Apple that guarantees the safety and retrievability of your photographs, even if that your device is lost or the hardware fails.

- **Easy Accessibility and Convenience**

Every Apple device gives you access to your complete photo library, regardless of where you are. You won't have to manually transfer your images because iCloud will automatically sync and save them for you. This will ensure that you have smooth access to your photos anywhere you go.

- **Optimizing Storage**

As a result of iCloud's clever management of space, storage is optimized, and your device is protected from becoming overcrowded. The most recent photographs are preserved in high resolution, while older photographs are saved as thumbnails with a lower resolution. This allows for the most efficient use of storage space.

Making use of iCloud for photo management not only improves the safety of your digital life but also makes it easier to manage your digital information. However, keep in mind that in order to access your iCloud images whenever and wherever you choose, you will need a reliable internet connection.

How to remove duplicate photos on your Mac

Despite the fact that we appreciate your enthusiasm for your photo collection, we believe that it is not the best idea to keep duplicates. There is a great probability that duplicate photographs may be overlooked. For this reason, it is strongly suggested that you make use of a third-party application, such as **a duplicate photos finder,** in order to swiftly sort through and get rid of duplicates.

In order to achieve the best possible outcomes, we recommend use **MacKeeper's Duplicates Finder.** This powerful application analyzes your Mac in a short amount of time to locate duplicate photos, images that are identical to one another, and unnecessary files, making it simple to delete them. An even greater feature is that it provides a free edition, which enables you to evaluate its capabilities before committing to using it.

Launching the MacKeeper app on your device is all that is required to make use of the Duplicates Finder feature of MacKeeper. Access the Duplicates Finder by going to the **Cleaning tab,** which is found in the left panel of the interface. The application will begin by performing a comprehensive scan of your Mac, after which it will provide you with a detailed list of duplicates that it identified.

To access the Similar Photos category, select the box that is adjacent to it. To remove the selected items, select the button that is located at the bottom of the screen and click on it.

It is now possible to clear your Mac Air M3 of the clutter caused by duplicate photos, and the entire procedure may be finished in a matter of minutes.

FAQs

1. When I use Finder on my Mac, why am I unable to view photos?

It is highly possible that the Pictures category is not selected to appear in the sidebar of Finder on your Mac, particularly if your photographs are not being displayed in the Finder application. A solution to this problem is as follows:

2. If I have a Mac, how can I get pictures to display in the Finder?

You will need to manually add the Pictures category to the sidebar in Finder on your Mac device in order to make sure that your pictures are displayed in the Finder application. Take the following actions:

- Launch the **Finder application**.
- After selecting "Finder" from the menu that appears in the upper-left corner of the screen, choose "Preferences."

- You may find the "Pictures" section by scrolling down the Favorites list.
- To enable it, check the box that is located next to it.

You should now see the "Pictures" option in the sidebar of Finder.

3. Do photos that are imported remain on the Mac?

It is true that the photographs library on your Mac is where all the photographs that you import are automatically saved. On the other hand, you have the option to store them in a different folder or on an external hard drive, and you will still be able to view them in Photos on your Mac system. You may locate photographs that have been imported by going to photographs > Imports.

4. How can you locate photos that have been hidden on a Mac?

The process of discovering images that are hidden on your Mac is simple. Take the following actions:

- Select Photos > View > Show Hidden Photo Album from the menu bar.
- The "Hidden" option can be found on the left panel.
- You can choose the picture that you want to show.
- Make sure to select "Unhide 1 Photo."

The Library will now display your photo in the same manner as any other photo.

CHAPTER TEN

Saving your MacBook Air M3 battery

It has been a few years since you started using your Mac, and you have just noticed that the battery is not keeping its charge as well as it once did. In order to prevent your new Mac device from dying on you, it is becoming increasingly inconvenient to always carry your charger around with you.

The lifespan of a MacBook is normally between five and seven years, although this can vary depending on a number of different circumstances. MacBooks are built to be quite durable. It is possible that problems with the battery life of your Mac, which falls within that age range, may not necessarily indicate that it is time to purchase a new device.

Before we get into potential remedies, however, it is crucial to address the background operations that may be draining your battery in an unnecessary manner. Many applications start up immediately when your Mac starts up, which might reduce the amount of time your battery lasts. It is possible to dramatically enhance performance and battery economy by efficiently managing these startup components.

A step-by-step method to managing the procedures that occur when your Mac starts up is as follows:

- To install MacKeeper on your Mac, download it.

- A scan can be started by clicking the **Start Scan button** after you have navigated to the **Login Items section** located on the left-hand side of the screen.

- Examine the list of programs/apps that are activated when the computer starts up. To remove the items you have selected, select them and then click the "Remove Selected Items > Remove" button.

Notwithstanding the fact that Apple is constantly improving the hardware of the MacBook with each new version, the modifications that have been made to the battery technology are very limited. Therefore, before you rush to purchase a new Mac, you should think about confronting the problem with the battery head-on.

In order to maximize the performance and battery life of your MacBook, follow these instruction steps.

Check your MacBook's battery percentage

It is not possible to extend the life of your MacBook Air M3 by reviewing the percentage of its battery. Estimating the amount of time that is still available on your Mac, on the other hand, can be useful because it could provide you with information about how much longer you can use it before it runs out.

Simply clicking on the **battery icon** that is situated in the upper-right hand corner of the screen will allow you to view the current percentage of the battery. In the event that the battery is low, it is advisable to close any applications that are not necessary, such as the Music app, in order to avoid unexpected shutdowns.

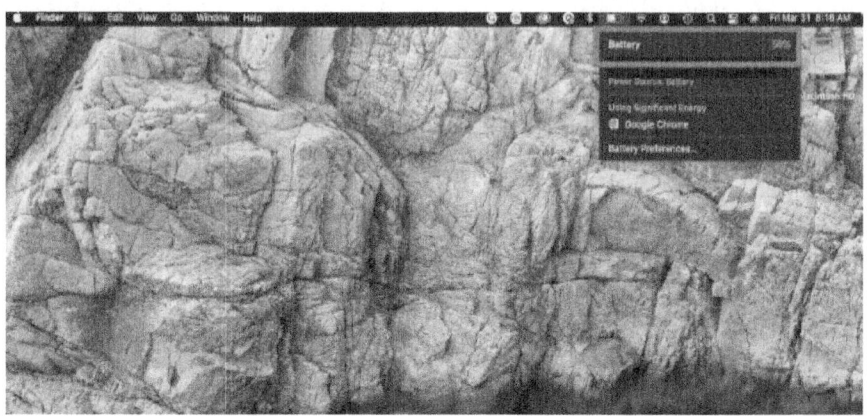

Check your MacBook's battery health

Assessing the condition of the battery in your MacBook is the next step in your process. When compared to older Macs that are powered by Intel, the battery of your Mac is likely to be in better condition if it is either brand new or equipped with an M3 chip. If that you have owned your Mac for a number of years, inherited it, or purchased it used, this information will prove to be really beneficial. Having an understanding of the capacity of the battery in your Mac enables you to keep it in good health.

Take the following procedures to determine the condition of the battery in your new MacBook device:

- Click on the **battery symbol** that is situated in the upper-right hand corner of the screen of your Mac, and then select "Battery Preferences."
- Select the "Battery" tab located on the left-hand side of the screen, and then proceed to click on the "Battery Health" option. Undertaking this step will cause a pop-up window to appear, which will display information regarding the current state of your Mac's battery as well as its maximum capacity.

- Even if the condition of the battery in your Mac appears to be poor, you should not immediately start thinking about replacing it. There are a variety of approaches that may be taken to extend the lifespan of your Mac charger.

Update to the latest macOS

When it comes to fixing bugs and addressing security vulnerabilities, the operating system of your laptop is absolutely necessary for ensuring the safety of your computer or laptop. On the other hand, it also makes a substantial contribution to further optimizing the performance of your gadget.

Using an outdated version of macOS might have a negative impact on your Mac, including the battery life of your device. Keeping your macOS up to date is absolutely necessary if you want to extend the amount of time that your MacBook's battery can last.

To upgrade the operating software on your Mac, the following actions need to be taken:

- First and foremost, access Software Update by navigating to **System Preferences.**
- Click the "Update Now" button if there are any available updates. In general, you will come across possibilities such as the macOS Catalina, Monterey, or Big Sur operating systems.

How to Use Safari instead of Chrome

Chrome, which has more than three billion users, is widely considered to be the best browser available. It is recognized for its speed, efficiency, and user-friendly layout. However, because of its high resource usage, it can quickly deplete the battery of your computer, making it less than ideal for MacBook owners who are considering ways to reduce their power consumption.

When this occurs, switching to Safari, which is the default web browser for Macs, is an attractive alternative to consider exploring. In spite of the fact that Safari's user interface can be different from Chrome's, you shouldn't let this deter you; Safari provides a streamlined and pleasurable surfing experience that is available to all users.

Use auto-brightness

If you increase the brightness of the screen on your Mac device, the battery life of the device will decrease. Additionally, the longer your screen stays bright, the greater the amount of power that is drawn from your battery. On your Mac, turning on the auto-brightness feature can reduce the amount of power that is drawn from the battery, so extending its lifespan.

The following actions need to be taken in order to activate auto-brightness on your Mac:

- To change the display, go to the **System Preferences menu.**
- The Display tab should be selected.

- You should select the option that says "Automatically adjust brightness."

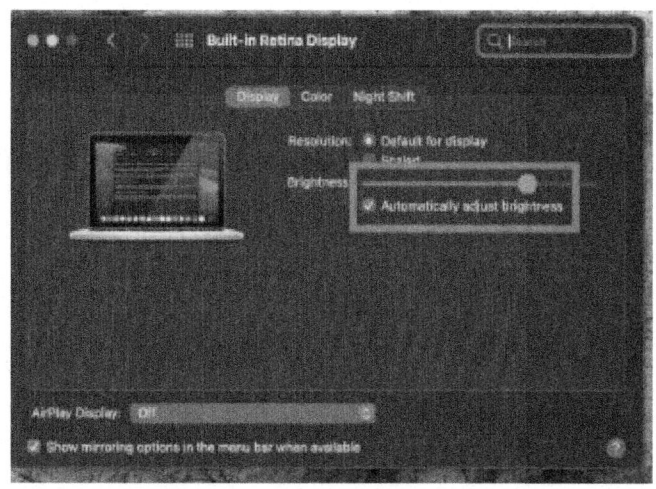

Disable Wi-Fi, Bluetooth, and AirDrop when not in use

What is the frequency with which you make use of Wi-Fi, Bluetooth, and AirDrop throughout the course of your day? Even though that it is probably not very often, these features have a tendency to be enabled without any thought being given to them. There is no incentive to keep these functions engaged unless they are absolutely necessary for the responsibilities you perform on a daily basis. It is possible to extend the battery life of your Mac by turning them off.

On the other hand, it is essential to keep in mind that turning off Bluetooth also turns off the Continuity function that Apple offers. It is because of this that you will no longer have the ability to share information between your Apple devices in a seamless manner, such as between your Mac and your iPhone.

On your Mac, you can deactivate Wi-Fi, Bluetooth, and AirDrop by following the instructions that are listed below:

- **Wi-Fi:** To turn off Wi-Fi on your Mac, first click on the icon that symbolizes Wi-Fi, which is situated in the upper-right hand corner of the screen?
- **Bluetooth:** Activate Bluetooth by clicking on the icon that is located to the left of the Wi-Fi icon, and then turn Bluetooth off by using the toggle switch.

- **Airdrop:** When using AirDrop, go to the Finder menu and pick AirDrop. After that, select "Allow me to be discovered by," and then select "No one."

Customize battery preferences

By allowing you to quickly reset your battery choices, Apple gives you the ability to extend the amount of time that your device's battery can last. Adjusting the brightness of the screen when it is powered by the battery and configuring the display on your Mac to turn off can significantly extend the amount of time that the battery will last.

If you want to customize the settings for your Mac's battery, follow these steps:

- Open the **System Preferences menu,** and then go to the Battery section.
- Select the box that is located next to the phrase "Slightly dim the display while on battery power."

- Move the slider that is located under the heading "Turn display off after" to the left and choose a period that is suitable for your preferences. This will result in additional conservation. By choosing a shorter length, you will achieve better results in terms of preserving the life of the battery.

Clean your Mac

If you don't realize that you're accumulating superfluous files on your Mac, you may be putting strain on your battery, which will eventually result in lower performance. It is possible to lessen this pressure and protect the life of your battery by cleaning your Mac on a regular basis.

It is highly recommended that you make use of the Safe Cleanup tool that is included in MacKeeper. This tool is meant to safely and effectively eliminate any clutter that may be present on your Mac. If you want to use it, follow these steps:

- Download MacKeeper, then go to **the Safe Cleanup section** on the left sidebar of the interface.

- Start a scan by clicking on the **Start Scan button**, and then give MacKeeper permission to evaluate your computer.

- After the scan is finished, you should look over the rubbish files that were noticed. You can get rid of them by clicking the **Clean Junk Files button** if you believe that they are not necessary.

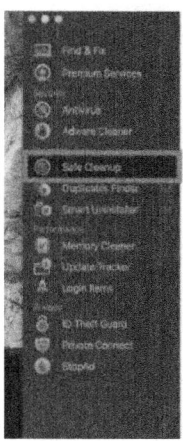

Turn off Turbo Boost

Turbo Boost is a built-in feature that can be found in Macs that are powered by Intel. Its purpose is to improve the performance of your Mac by simultaneously operating in the background. The tasks that you are completing will determine whether or not it is activated automatically; however, you have the option to disable it in order to save additional battery life.

Simply follow these instructions in order to establish whether or not your Mac is equipped with Turbo Boost:

- Select "About This Mac" from the Apple menu option.
- You should add the word "specs" to the end of the search query once you have copied and pasted the first line of the requirements into Google Search results.

- Choose the search result that is associated with Apple Support (https://support.apple.co m).
- Examine the section titled "Processor." This indicates that your Mac is capable of supporting the Turbo Boost feature. Then you should move on to the following section.

Also, by disabling Turbo Boost, you can save the battery life of your device by following these steps:

- Launch the application after downloading the Turbo Boost Switcher program.
- Simply open the Turbo Boost Switcher by navigating to it.
- After clicking on the lightning icon, select the option that says "**Disable Turbo Boost**."

Enable automatic graphics switching on MacBook

Dual graphics systems are available on the MacBook Air M3 device. One of these systems is designed to maximize power efficiency (integrated graphics processor), while the other is designed to maximize performance (discrete graphics processor), despite the fact that it consumes more battery power.

In order to reduce your power consumption, you can turn on automatic graphics switching. In this manner:

- To activate the Energy Saver, go to the **System Preferences menu**.
- Choose the option to switch graphics automatically.

Shut down your Mac at night

Simply putting your Mac to sleep, which still uses up battery life, is all that happens when you close it. When you are not using your Mac, especially overnight or during longer periods of non-use, make sure to turn it off. This will ensure that your battery lasts as long as possible.

Disconnect accessories you aren't using

The drain on a battery might be caused by devices that are connected via USB. It is important to remember to detach them from your Mac after using them in order to extend the life of the battery.

Quit apps you aren't using

The power consumption of applications that are left operating in the background continues. For the sake of preserving battery life, make it a habit to close applications that you are no longer using.

Prevent apps from launching automatically on startup

When you power up your device, applications that start up automatically can put unnecessary burden on your battery. Make use of the Login Items feature of MacKeeper to manage which applications start up when the computer is turned on, so preserving the battery life.

Plug your MacBook when charging connected devices

Every time you use your Mac to charge an external device, such your iPhone, it uses up some of the power that your Mac has available. To guarantee that your MacBook's battery lasts as long as possible, you should make sure that it is connected to a power source even when you are charging other devices.

Use Activity Monitor to see battery-hogging apps

By making use of Activity Monitor, you can determine which applications are depleting your battery:

- Pressing the **Command key** and the spacebar simultaneously will open the Spotlight search window. Once it is open, type "Activity Monitor" into the search bar and choose it from the list of results.

- To access the Energy tab under Activity Monitor, navigate to the tab.
- Determine the applications that are spending a considerable amount of energy.
- Select the application that you want to close, click the **X icon** that is situated at the top of the window, and then click "Quit." This will help you save valuable battery life.

Plug your MacBook during intensive tasks

The battery life of your MacBook Air M3 may be negatively impacted by labor-intensive activities such as downloading huge files and streaming video content. When you are using your Mac extensively, make sure that it is plugged in so that the battery is not overworked. This will help lessen the issue. In the event that the battery on your Mac is not charging, you should also become familiar with the methods involved in troubleshooting.

Use the original charger and cable

Refrain from using chargers not made by Apple, especially with devices featuring a MagSafe port, as this could potentially harm your Mac's battery. If you want to keep your battery in the best possible condition, you should only use the charger and cable that came with the device or that you purchased from an authorized Apple Store.

Keep your Mac's battery healthy with MacKeeper

By implementing behaviors that are beneficial to the health of the battery, you can extend the longevity of your MacBook. Make use of MacKeeper to investigate a variety of strategies for preserving the life of the battery.

It is important to regularly examine and manage the Login Items on your MacBook in order to improve the efficiency of the startup process and the longevity of the battery. This includes the following:

- Choosing which programs will run when the computer is first started up. With a centralized location, monitoring and managing all of the startup elements is possible.
- In order to improve battery performance, it is necessary to identify and eliminate potentially hazardous processes.

CHAPTER ELEVEN

Download and Install Apps not from

App store

There may be situations in which you would rather download applications directly to your Mac from sources other than the App Store, despite the fact that the macOS App Store provides a method of installing applications that is both convenient and secure. One possible explanation for this is that the app in question is not currently available in the store, or that there is a particular version that can only be obtained from the official website.

However, while downloading software from sources other than the App Store, it is essential to take security into consideration. In spite of the fact that malware has been discovered in apps that are not part of the App Store in the past, apps that are not part of the App Store represent a possibly bigger danger and may also cause compatibility concerns.

This chapter will walk you through the process of downloading applications onto your MacBook Air M3 from sources other than the App Store in a secure manner.

Before You Get Started;

It is highly recommended that you have antivirus protection installed on your device if you intend to download software from a source other than the App Store. MacKeeper provides a full suite of utilities, which includes capabilities for optimization, cleaning, and privacy protection, as well as on-demand and real-time antivirus protection.

It is imperative that any applications that have been downloaded be scanned with the Antivirus feature of MacKeeper before they are launched.

- After opening MacKeeper, select the "Antivirus" option.
- The scanning procedure can be started by selecting the "Start Scan" button.
- The virus that MacKeeper has identified should be selected from the list if it is found.
- To isolate the malware that has been found, click the "Move to Quarantine" button.
- You may explore the entire range of possibilities that MacKeeper has to offer by giving it a try today.

How to download apps from anywhere on Mac

Apple is committed to adhering to the requirements that govern the admission of applications in the App Store. These guidelines are designed to protect users and maintain high quality standards. Assuming that an application does not fulfill these requirements or the developer chooses not to participate in the store, customers are still able to obtain the application by downloading it straight from the official website of the developer or from other reliable sources.

Here are a few well-known applications that may be downloaded via non-App Store sources:

- VLC (video player)
- GrandPerspective (disk space visualizer)
- Audacity (audio editor)
- OpenEmu (games emulator)

Following the acquisition of applications for your Mac from third-party sources, the subsequent step is to install those applications. Let's investigate options for achieving this goal.

How to install software on Mac not from App Store

In most cases, the process of installing an application that was obtained from a source other than the App Store is uncomplicated. In most cases, you may simply drag the application or folder into the Applications folder on your computer. However, there are some that may come with installers.

To install an application that is not available in the App Store, follow these steps:

- The application can be downloaded from the website of the developer or from any reliable source.
- Make use of MacKeeper or another reliable antivirus program in order to check the downloaded file for any forms of malware.

- If the file that you downloaded is a zip archive, you can unzip it by double-clicking on it. A DMG file can be mounted in Finder by double-clicking on it, and then the application can be moved to the Applications folder by dragging it.
- To begin the installation process, double-click the PKG installer that is included with the file. This will allow you to continue with the process.

How to allow apps downloaded from anywhere on Mac

It is simple to install applications that are not available through the App Store on your Mac Air M3 device; but, the Gatekeeper security function may restrict the running of these applications unless you give permission for them to run. Either on a case-by-case basis or by allowing all downloaded applications to execute automatically, you have the ability to handle this.

- Let us assume that System Preferences is open, simply close it.
- Open Terminal by going to Applications > Utilities and then clicking on it.
- Simply press the **Return key** after entering "sudo spctl --master-disable."
- Press the **Return key** after you have provided your admin password.
- Once again, open System Preferences and select "Anywhere" from the list of options under "Allow apps downloaded from."

How to open apps on Mac not from App Store

In spite of the fact that you have disabled downloaded applications in the System Settings, you are still able to execute them separately. It is possible that your MacBook Air M3 will ask you to verify that you intend to run an untrusted application, or it may completely prevent you from doing so. If this occurs, you will be required to use a different method in order to start the application.

To execute particular applications that are not available on the App Store, follow these steps:

- Click and hold the app that has not been verified. Click the "Open" button if you are prompted with the question "Are you sure you want to open it?"

- If you are unable to access this option, you will be presented with the decision to either delete the application from your device or to cancel opening it. Simply select "Cancel".

- You should then go to **the System Settings menu** and select **Privacy & Security.** Scroll down until you come across a notification that says the application has been blocked. To access your administrative password, click the "Open Anyway" button. Simply select "Open" from the accompanying pop-up window.

- Choose "Open" from the context menu that appears when you right-click on the application rather than going to the System Settings menu.

- A pop-up message will appear in the same manner for you. To start the application, click the "Open" button.

From this point on, you will not be subjected to any warnings when you open the application as you normally would.

How to uninstall software on Mac not from App Store

When it comes to the App Store: The method of uninstalling applications is the same regardless of whether they were downloaded via the App Store or from a third-party source. Let's say that the application comes with its own folder and a file to remove it, you should run that file. If that is not the case, you can easily remove the application from the Applications folder by dragging it to the Trash followed by emptying it.

Apps that have been deleted may, however, leave behind leftover files that are dispersed throughout the system of your device. The process of manually locating and removing these leftovers is not impossible, but it can be a time-consuming process. Consider use MacKeeper to delete applications in an effective manner while also guaranteeing that no residual files are left behind. This will help to streamline the procedure further.

Here is how to make use of the Smart Uninstaller that comes with MacKeeper:

- Start up MacKeeper and choose the **Smart Uninstaller option.**

- After that, simply click the "Start Scan" button.

- Following the completion of the scan, select the application that you want to delete and then click the "Remove Selected" button.

- Select "Remove" from the pop-up that appears after that.

The application that we provide will be completely removed from your MacBook Air M3, and no lingering files will be left behind.

Note: Be wary of applications that are not available via the App Store. Although there are a great number of outstanding apps that can be downloaded from sources other than the App Store, it is essential to take caution. Always download from official websites, use MacKeeper's Smart Uninstaller to delete applications when they are no longer required, and make sure that all downloads are scanned with MacKeeper's Antivirus software during the process.

If the applications you require are offered by the App Store, it is recommended that you download them from that location. In any other case, you should maintain vigilance and attempt to navigate safely.

CHAPTER TWELVE

Siri

Siri is Apple's voice assistant, and it is integrated into almost all the company's products, including Mac computers, in a seamless manner. Through the use of voice commands, users are able to carry out tasks like as looking for files and modifying the settings of the system.

If you are already familiar with Siri on your iPhone or iPad, you might find it advantageous to activate and make use of Siri on your new MacBook Air M3 device as well. In the following chapter, we will walk you through the process of using Siri on your new device.

What is Siri?

Apple's digital voice assistant, Siri, is widely used on iOS devices, specifically iPhones and iPads. In 2016, it began to integrate with Macs, and since then, it has gained a significant amount of popularity. Siri provides a wide range of features, such as the ability to search for files, modify system settings, and provide weather updates, among other advantages.

It is possible that you will be prompted to enable Siri while you are installing a new version of macOS or when you are setting up your Mac for the first time. It is possible to activate it using the System Settings in macOS if it is not already activated.

How to enable Siri

Siri is available in the new MacBook Air M3 device and succeeding versions of the operating system.

Following these steps will allow you to activate Siri on your new device;

- Launch the **System Preferences application** on your Mac, and then choose the 'Siri & Spotlight' option from the sidebar.
- Siri can be activated by toggling the 'Enable Ask Siri' switch.

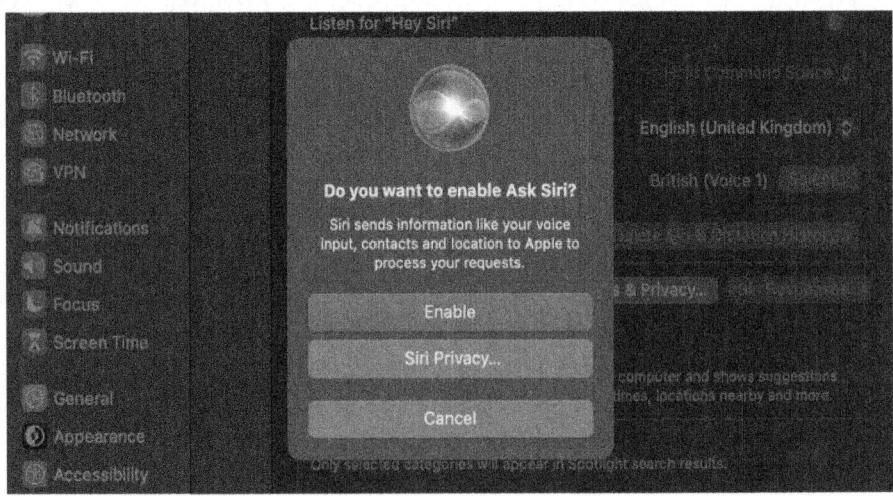

- You will also need to enable the feature known as "Allow Siri when locked" in order to use Siri for voice commands. It is possible that Siri will ask you to repeat a few phrases in order to train itself to identify your voice.

A successful activation of Siri has been completed on your new Mac device. On the same preferences page, you have the ability to further adjust parameters such as language and voice (including accent).

How to activate Siri

Once you have activated Siri on your new Mac device, you will have a number of different choices to call upon it. It is the voice command approach that is used the most frequently; all you have to do is say "Hey Siri." You also have the option of accessing Siri by using a keyboard shortcut or by clicking the Siri button that is situated in the menu bar of your Mac.

Additionally, if you would rather not speak out loud, you have the option of using the Type to Siri feature. We will examine each of these approaches in turn in the following paragraphs.

- **Using the "Hey Siri" Voice Command:**

The "Hey Siri" command is the most common way to start Siri on your device. It is also the most popular approach. Navigate to the Siri & Spotlight section of the System Preferences menu in order to activate this option.

After the feature has been activated, your Mac will begin to listen for your voice and will activate Siri when it detects the command. In order for Siri to identify your voice, she will ask you to say a few words while you are setting it up. Simply uttering the phrase "Hey Siri" when the setup process is complete will cause the Siri window to appear in the upper-right hand corner, ready to receive your orders.

- **From the Menu Bar**

As an alternative, you can activate Siri by hitting the Siri button that is situated in the top-right corner of the menu bar. If you are having problems finding it, it is located next to the date for your convenience. Simply clicking on this button will immediately bring up the Siri interface, which will enable you to communicate with your personal assistant.

- **Using a keyboard shortcut**

You can also activate Siri by using a keyboard shortcut, which may be configured in the Siri section of System Preferences. This is another way to activate Siri. The Keyboard Shortcut menu allows you to select from a selection of pre-set shortcuts or to create your own. Using this user-friendly way, you will be able to call Siri into existence simply from your keyboard.

- **Type to Siri**

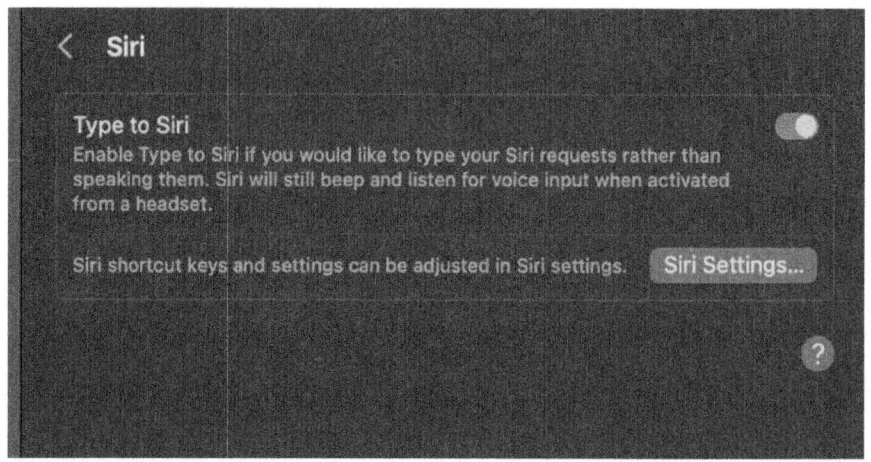

You can activate "Type to Siri" in the Accessibility section of **System Preferences** if you would rather not use voice commands. This feature is available for people who would rather not use voice instructions.

By activating this function, you will be able to type your Siri orders rather than uttering them verbally. It is very helpful to have this option available in public places, where it may not be the best idea to speak to Siri.

What to use Siri for?

On your new MacBook Air M3 device, Siri functions as a multifunctional voice assistant that is able to easily carry out a variety of tasks. Do you need to find a specific folder or file? This eliminates the need to travel through Spotlight because all you have to do is ask Siri. Setting Siri to search for files gives you the ability to customize your search preferences by allowing you to designate certain folders inside the System Settings > Siri menu.

As an illustration, you can instruct Siri to "find documents created last week," which will promptly provide you with results that are pertinent to your inquiry. In addition to searching for files, Siri provides a wide range of other services, such as reading emails, providing weather updates, conducting Google searches, and a great deal more.

The capability of Siri to drag and drop items is a function that is extremely helpful. Imagine being able to ask Siri to identify a particular image or file, and then being able to quickly drag it into your email in order to send it as an attachment. In comparison to the procedure of manually looking for and adding files through Finder, this makes the process more efficient.

It is possible to improve your productivity by incorporating Siri into your everyday routine. By eliminating the need for additional applications, Siri makes it easier to perform tasks such as setting reminders or alarms. In spite of the fact that the "Hey Siri" voice command is the most common way for users to activate Siri, there are other ways to activate Siri, such as using the menu bar, or a keyboard shortcut that may be customized on your Mac.

CHAPTER THIRTEEN

Apple ID

How often do you find yourself awestruck by the seamless synchronization of settings and preferences across all of your Apple devices, including your Mac, iPhone, and other Apple products? The Apple ID login, which functions as your unique Apple account within its ecosystem, is responsible for making this extraordinary coherence possible.

A user can create a new account, change their password, and even delete their account permanently with an Apple ID. These are just some of the much functionality that an Apple ID provides. Examine the possible activities that are associated with your Apple ID in further detail by delving deeper into the detailed chapter that is provided below.

What's my Apple ID?

Apple Music, the App Store, iMessage, FaceTime, iCloud, and other vital services are all accessible through your Apple ID, which acts as a gateway to the Apple ecosystem. Also, your Apple ID stores your preferences and settings, and it grants access to these services. It is of critical importance in ensuring that users have a consistent experience across all Apple devices.

It is highly likely that you have been presented with a multitude of prompts encouraging you to create an Apple ID, even if you only possess a single Apple product.

The good news is that establishing a new Apple ID is not only highly recommended but also very simple, regardless of whether you choose to do so through iTunes, your web browser, or the App Store.

You will be required to supply crucial information, including the following, regardless of the method that you choose to use.

- Email address (which will serve as your Apple ID)
- Name Date of Birth
- Use of a password
- Billing Address

How to create Apple ID using different methods

If you have recently loaded a new version of iTunes, you will be prompted to identify yourself by making use of your Apple ID. The option to create a new Apple ID will also be presented to you in response to this notification.

For individuals who have used iTunes in the past, there are a few additional actions that need to be taken in order to create your Apple ID:

- To sign in, go to the menu bar at the top of the page and select Account > Sign In. It is necessary for you to sign out of any other accounts that are currently logged in before you can proceed.

- Select "Create New Apple ID" from the menu.
- Also, fill out the form carefully by including all the required information.

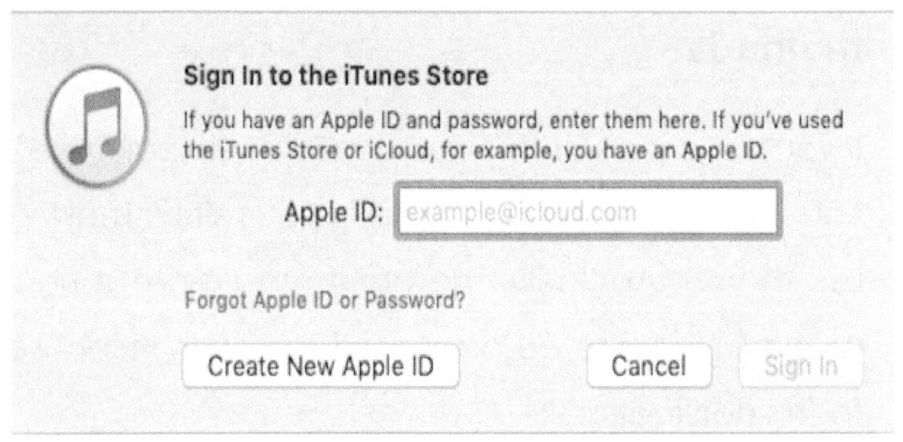

How to reset password you forgot

A few of the reasons why you might need to change your Apple password include the following: you may have forgotten the password for your Apple ID, or it may have been compromised. Alternately, you can have the impression that another individual has acquired access to your account.

There is a basic method for changing the password associated with your Apple ID, regardless of the reason:

- By selecting **Sign In from** the Accounts menu in iTunes, the App Store, or the Apple ID website, you may see your account information.
- Choose the option to "Forgot Apple ID or Password."
- You will need to enter all of the required information in order to reset your Apple password.

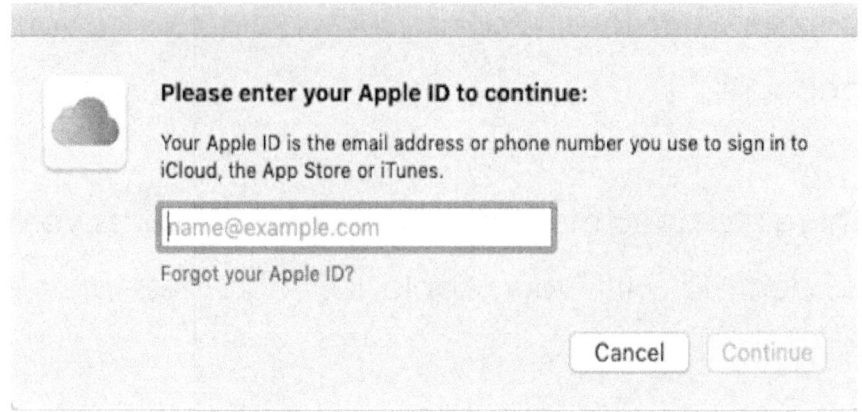

How to change Apple ID on Mac

It is possible to make changes to all the information associated with your Apple ID, including the email address that you use to access your Apple account:

- To access the appleid.apple.com website, open your web browser.
- Enter your Apple ID and password to join the service.
- To edit your account, select the **Edit button**.
- Modify your Apple ID with the email address you are currently using.

- After entering the new email address, select the **Continue button** to change your Apple ID.

You should be aware that if you attempt to log in to your Apple account with an incorrect password an excessive number of times, your account may be locked for a period of twenty-four hours. Therefore, if you are experiencing problems checking in, you should choose to reset your password by using the option to Forget Apple ID or Password before you are locked out of your account. In that case, you will be need to wait until the next day in order to modify your Apple ID.

How to delete Apple ID

You won't believe this, but up until very recently, it was not possible to delete your Apple ID. You had the option to deactivate it, which was essentially equivalent to uninstalling it; however, Apple would still keep your information even if you did so.

On the other hand, Apple introduced a data and privacy site in 2018, which gives users the ability to modify the information they supply with the firm, including the ability to completely delete their ID.

Take some time to consider the repercussions of deleting your Apple ID before you actually go ahead and do it. First things first, you need to make sure that your files are backed up. To complete the process of removing your Apple ID from your Mac, you must first deauthorize iTunes and then sign out of iCloud.

How to backup your files

The deletion of your Apple ID comes with a number of potential dangers. For example, it is possible to lose some files, contacts, and syncs; in addition, it is likely that you will lose access to the applications and music that you have purchased using your Apple ID.

Before you erase your Apple ID, it is vital to create a backup of your files. Disk Drill is the greatest application for creating a complete backup of your contents on a hard drive. If something goes wrong, you can then make use of this backup to restore your files into their original state. You also have the option of using a cloud storage application such as Dropshare in order to guarantee that you will continue to have access to all of your essential files even after you have made significant modifications to your Mac.

A guide to using Disk Drill to create backups of your Mac

If something goes wrong, it should be a no-brainer for you to back up your files so that you can restore them. The application known as **Disk Drill** is a robust and user-friendly program that is capable of generating backup disk images. These images can be utilized to restore your Mac to its previous state of excellence.

Having Disk Drill installed and an external drive (such as a USB thumb drive) ready to start, the following steps should be taken:

- First and foremost, launch the Disk Drill.
- Choose Backup > Backup into DMG-image from the menu at the top of the menu.
- If you are backing up your Mac, the drive you select will be your primary hard drive. If you are backing up another disk, select the drive instead. Click the Backup button in your selection once it has been highlighted.
- Make sure to give your backup file a name and specify the location where it will be saved. The location of your external drive should be in this area. Make sure that your backup is not saved on the same drive that you are saving the backup to.

Following the completion of the Disk Drill saving process, you will be able to mount a secure duplicate of your Mac by using the application.

Tips for using Dropshare to create backups of your Mac

Dropshare, in contrast to other recovery tools, is an excellent method for backing up particular files that you do not want those files to be affected by modifications made to your Mac. You can use Dropshare to save your vital documents or media assets rather of creating a full backup of your computer. This will save you time during the process.

Dropshare is distinguished from other cloud storage services by the fact that, in addition to providing its own cloud storage that may be usedd with the application, it can also be simply configured to use other cloud storage providers such as Dropbox, Google Drive, Amazon S3, and others. The software offers a great deal of versatility.

You may back up certain files on your Mac by downloading Dropshare, which will prevent you from losing even a little amount of storage space.

After you have installed and configured Dropshare's cloud storage, all you need to do is drag and drop the files you wish to back up into the Dropshare client. The client will then upload the files to the cloud, ensuring that they are protected from any modifications you make to your Mac.

After your files have been backed up in their entirety, you will be able to proceed with the deletion of your Apple ID.

iTunes should be de-authorized on your Mac

The authorization of iTunes, which grants you access to the iTunes store and all cloud purchases, is accomplished through the use of your Apple ID. Before you delete your Apple ID, you need make sure that iTunes is deauthorized. This will allow you to link your Apple ID to a different account in the future:

- Select Account > Deauthorize from the menu. On the menu bar, this computer is located.
- Enter the password for your Apple ID, and then click the Deauthorize button to confirm.

Next, log out of your iCloud account on your Mac:

- Launch System Preferences > iCloud.
- The bottom-left corner of the iCloud settings pane is where you will find the Sign Out button.

Final step: delete your Apple ID:

- Register for an account with your Apple ID by going to appleid.apple.com.
- Go to the section that is labeled Devices and scroll down.
- On the list of devices, locate your Mac, and then click the **Remove button.**
- As many devices as are required, repeat the process.

How to delete your Apple ID account

Before beginning the process of deletion, you should first create a backup of your Apple ID and then remove it from your Mac. Whenever you are prepared:

- In your web browser, navigate to the privacy.apple.com website.
- To access your account, use your Apple ID and password.
- Within the box labeled "Delete Your Account," select the "Get Started" option.
- It is necessary to select the proper option from the pulldown menu in order to provide an explanation for the deletion of your Apple ID login.
- In order to receive information on the status of your account, simply provide a contact method, and then click the Continue button.
- For the purpose of verifying your identification to Apple support, you should write down the access code.

- After being prompted, enter the access code, and then proceed.

Your Apple ID account will not be removed immediately if you click the **Delete Account button** and approve the deletion. Apple will begin a verification procedure that will last for one week before removing your account and all of the data linked with it. During this time, you will have the opportunity to change your mind and cancel your subscription using your access code. In the event that the verification procedure is completed, your account will be deleted permanently.

Your Apple ID is an essential component of your Apple experience, as you are probably aware by this point. You will have the ability to effortlessly create, modify, and delete your Apple ID if you follow the guide that was provided above. However, before you start with any modifications that cannot be undone, you must ensure that you have a complete backup of your Mac using Disk

Drill   or   a   partial   backup   using   Dropshare.

CHAPTER FOURTEEN

Using AirDrop on your Mac Device

AirDrop is the best option to go with if you are looking for a way that is both the quickest and most convenient for getting data transferred between two Apple devices. On this chapter, you will find instructions on how to activate and use AirDrop on your Mac, which will allow you to share images, documents, websites, and a variety of other things to other Apple devices in a smooth manner.

How to send files from your device using AirDrop

Wi-Fi and Bluetooth are used by AirDrop in order to build a wireless peer-to-peer connection. This connection makes it possible for users to seamlessly share files between two Apple devices. AirDrop is a handy file transfer service that has a range of around 10 meters, which is equivalent to approximately 30 feet (30 meters).

The seamless sharing of files is one of the most significant benefits of using AirDrop, and this benefit is present regardless of whether the recipient is a contact or not. Not only that, but every single file that is sent using AirDrop is completely encrypted, which guarantees both security and privacy.

- To begin the process of transferring files using AirDrop on your new Mac device, you must first click on the icon that represents the **Control Center**, which is situated in the upper-right hand corner of the menu bar. AirDrop can then be activated by selecting it from the menu. The activation of Bluetooth and Wi-Fi will take place immediately when AirDrop is enabled.
- Additionally, it is essential for the recipient to have AirDrop enabled on their Apple device

prior to receiving the message. Let just assume that they are not included in your contact list, they should proceed to toggle AirDrop on and then set it to the "Everyone" setting. Another option is to go to the **Finder menu**, then select **AirDrop,** then select **Allow me to be discovered by,** and finally select **Everyone.**

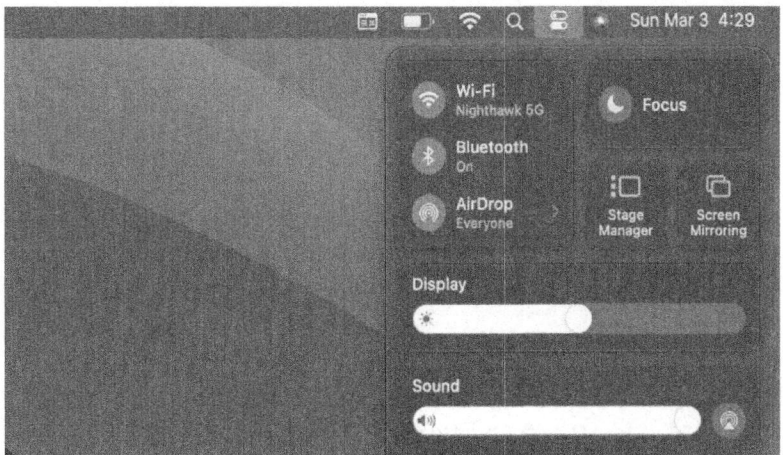

- Whenever you want to send a file, all you have to do is press Control and click on the file, and then select **Share > AirDrop** from the menu that appears. To use the AirDrop option within applications such as Preview, pick the

Share icon, which is shown as a box with an arrow pointing in its direction.

- Soon after the recipient has been chosen, the file will be transferred using AirDrop. Following this, the recipient is required to accept the file by hitting the "Accept" button on their device in order for the transfer to be successfully completed.

- Files can be sent via AirDrop in a number of different ways, including the Share > AirDrop technique, which involves dragging and dropping the files directly from Finder. After opening a second Finder window, select the file you want to transfer by navigating to Finder > AirDrop. This will allow you to view the receivers who are available for the transfer. It is possible to commence the transfer of the file by dragging and dropping it onto the contact of your choice within the AirDrop window.

How to receive files on your device using AirDrop

On your new MacBook Air M3 device, the method of receiving files over AirDrop is a straightforward one. Your Mac will send you a notification whenever a user of an Apple device in close proximity transmits a file once AirDrop has been enabled and set to the **Everyone setting**. After clicking the **Accept button,** you will be prompted to select the location where you would like the file to be transferred.

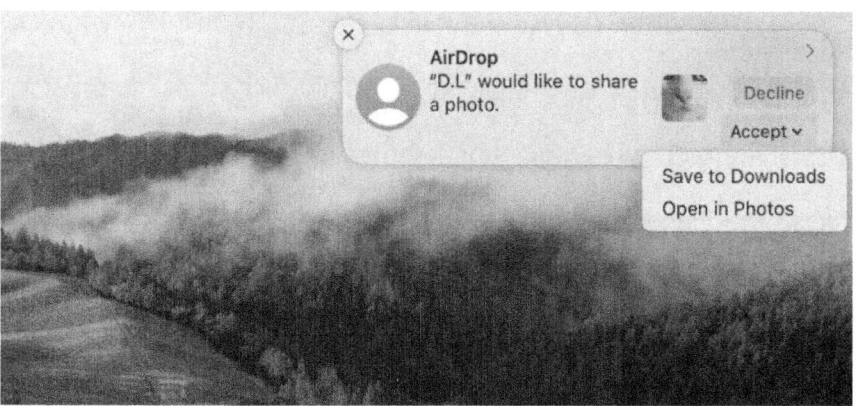

A number of users could be concerned about their privacy when receiving files with AirDrop because of the possibility of unexpected file transfers. You always have the choice to accept or deny the transfer before it begins, as was mentioned earlier in the sentence.

When two Apple devices are in close proximity to one another, such as in an office or a café, AirDrop is an effective technique for exchanging files between the two devices.

When it comes to file transfers, AirDrop is generally reliable; nevertheless, there are times when it can have some difficulties. On your Apple device, you are fortunate to have access to troubleshooting options that can quickly resolve issues that are associated with AirDrop. Other options for moving files between your Apple devices are also accessible in the event that distance proves to be an obstacle.

CHAPTER FIFTEEN

Security features built into your

MacBook Air M3

Apple's stringent safety protocols have earned the company a reputation for a long time. On the other hand, the explosion in popularity of MacBooks has attracted the attention of cybercriminals, which has led to an increase in the number of assaults on these devices.

As an illustration, a study conducted in 2021 found that the development of malware for macOS had skyrocketed by more than one thousand percent in the year 2020, with the finding of more than 674,273 new malware samples.

Acquiring knowledge of the security protocols used by macOS is essential for the protection of your data. It is important to keep in mind that the preventative actions you take will have a significant impact on the safety of your data. It is imperative that you take the initiative to become familiar with the security features of macOS. This will ensure that you take every possible step to strengthen your safety in the current digital world.

Instant Screen Auto-lock

Despite being one of the most straightforward security measures of macOS, the screen auto-lock feature is frequently disregarded. In order to achieve the highest possible level of efficiency, you should configure the "Require Password" setting to automatically activate "Immediately." This assures that your Mac user account will immediately log out anytime there is a brief period of inactivity on your Mac.

Imagine you are working in a cafe when you suddenly find yourself falling asleep. Because it prohibits anyone in the immediate vicinity from viewing sensitive information that is displayed on your screen, this feature becomes extremely important.

When you need to step away from your Mac in public or let us just assume that it is lost or stolen, the quick auto-lock serves as an essential security measure. While it might seem inconvenient at first glance, it's actually a highly valuable defense mechanism.

Putting Auto-Lock into action is as follows:

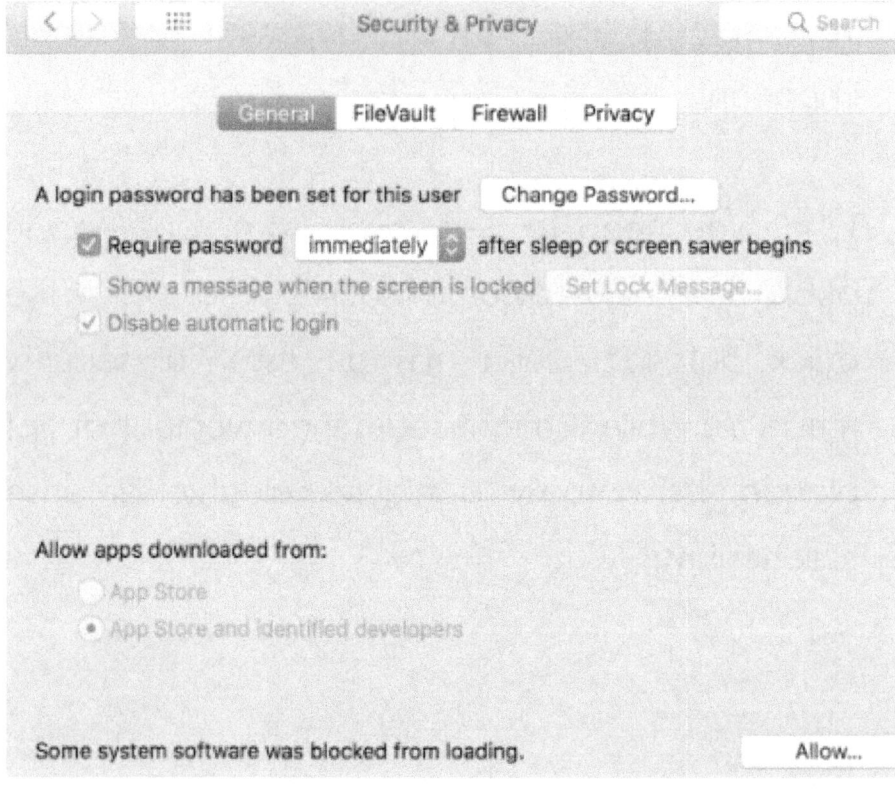

- Make sure to click on the **Apple menu icon.**
- Afterwards, go to System Preferences, and then select **Security & Privacy** from the menu.
- Select "Require Password" from the General menu, and then change the setting to "Immediately."

FileVault Encryption

FileVault is one of the most important security features of macOS, and it is especially important for protecting your MacBook in the event that it ever gets into the hands of someone who is not allowed to use it. Enabling FileVault will ensure that your hard drive is encrypted, making it unavailable to anyone who does not possess the specific decryption key.

In other words, even if an unauthorized person were to succeed in bypassing the password for your administrative account, they would still be unable to access any of the data that are considered to be of essential importance to you. Additionally, once a certain amount of time has passed, FileVault will automatically remove the decryption key from memory, which will further strengthen the protection of your data against any and all future intrusions.

Make sure to follow these steps in order to configure FileVault:

- First and foremost, select the Apple menu icon.
- After navigating to System Preferences, proceed to **Security & Privacy** to complete the process.
- Find the FileVault tab, and then click the button that says "Turn on FileVault."
- To generate a decryption key, you will need to follow the procedures that are given.

Additionally, we strongly recommend that you use FileVault to encrypt any external disks that are attached to your Mac by protecting them. If you attach an external drive, you can accomplish this by selecting the "Turn On FileVault" option for the drive.

Firmware Password

Setting up a firmware password for your Mac provides an additional layer of protection against hackers who are proficient in technology, hence enhancing the security of your Mac. When your Mac boots up in an unusual fashion, such as from a separate device, the recovery partition, or through a combination of startup keys, you will be forced to enter this password.

Creating a password for the firmware on an Intel Mac system:

- Activate the Mac Firmware Password Utility at this time.
- Also turn off your Mac.
- By holding down the Cmd and R keys at startup, you can boot into the recovery partition.
- Make your way to the Utilities menu.
- Choose either the Firmware Password Utility or the Startup Security Utility in the menu.

- Once you are prompted, select "Turn on Firmware Password" from the menu that appears.
- Also, provide a strong password that you will be able to recall.
- Restart your Mac by selecting the Apple menu option.

Because resetting the password for your firmware, in contrast to the password for your administrative account, is not a straightforward process, it is essential that you adhere to step 5. If you forget it, you will be required to go to an Apple Store with your Mac and providing proof of purchase in order to have it reset.

Mac Firewall

Installing a firewall is the first line of defense you have against any external dangers that may attempt to get access to your system. It is nevertheless recommended that you enable the firewall on your Mac, despite the fact that many internet routers already come with installed firewalls.

It is possible that disabling the firewall will make it easier to connect with other Apple devices; however, activating the firewall is still essential, particularly when connecting to public networks on a fairly regular basis.

Simply follow these instructions in order to activate your firewall:

- Proceed to **System Preferences** and then choose the **Security & Privacy** pane from the menu that appears.
- Make sure you select the Firewall tab.
- To unlock the settings, click the **lock symbol**, and then when requested, enter your administrator name and password (which are the same as the credentials you need to successfully log in to your Mac).

- By pressing the "Turn On Firewall" button, you can activate the firewall.
- Access the "Firewall Options" menu to make adjustments to the settings.

For an increased level of protection, you should think about using "Stealth Mode," which prevents your Mac from responding to port scans and connection attempts from unknown sources. This makes it more difficult for cybercriminals to locate your laptop.

XProtect Virus Scanner

XProtect is the name of the antivirus software that comes pre-installed on Macs, did you know that? When an application is launched for the first time or updated, it does a scan of the application and prevents any malware that is found from operating.

One of the advantages of XProtect is that it does not require any setting from the user and it functions without any interruptions in the background, providing protection to the fullest extent of its capabilities. You need only make sure that your operating system is always up to date, and you will be ready to go.

Nevertheless, it is essential to keep in mind that XProtect still has flaws that need to be addressed. According to MacWorld, it does not detect as many different types of malware as antivirus software that is specifically designed for Mac computers.

Craig Federighi, the Head of Software at Apple, admitted in 2021 that "the level of Mac malware is unacceptable," taking into account the fact that the number of reported Mac infections was more than the number of Windows infections.

Although XProtect does provide protection against malware, it is essential to be aware that it is not as thorough as some of the third-party Mac anti-malware software that is now available.

Due to the fact that there is frequently a trade-off between speed and protection, we recommend conducting research on the solutions that are the most suitable for your needs and selecting antivirus software that does not slow down your Mac.

App Sandboxing and Gatekeeper

App sandboxing and Gatekeeper are two examples of other useful security technologies that are included in macOS security features. These capabilities are aligned with Xprotect. System Integrity Protection (SIP) is a fundamental part of macOS, and both apps are integral components of SIP. They operate together to protect Mac computers from illegal code.

App Sandboxing does not offer complete protection against malicious software; nonetheless, it does considerably limit the capabilities of software that is specifically designed to cause harm. Application Sandboxing is a technique that restricts applications to particular parameters, so preventing them from accessing essential system files and folders. This helps to mitigate the possible damage that could be caused by unknown sources, such as malware.

On the other side, Gatekeeper is a defensive system that prevents users from installing software from developers who are not trusted. This defense mechanism is designed to protect users from dangerous apps. As a consequence of this, users are only able to acquire programs from reliable sources such as the App Store or from developers who have been identified, which results in an increased level of security.

In the event that certain security rules are not adhered to, a message may be triggered, which will alert users to the possibility of threats originating from unknown sources and malware.

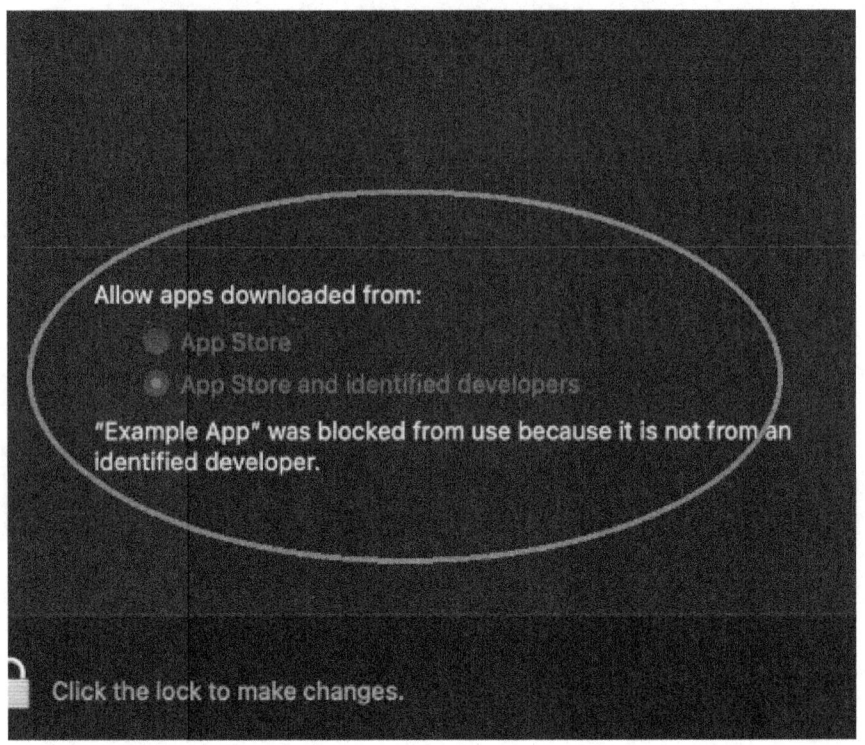

Allow apps downloaded from:

App Store

App Store and identified developers

"Example App" was blocked from use because it is not from an identified developer.

Click the lock to make changes.

These steps need to be taken in order to customize the Gatekeeper settings:

- Click on the **System Preferences** menu option.
- The General tab can be accessed after selecting the **Security & Privacy option.**
- Select the option that best suits your needs when it comes to downloading applications, whether it be from the "App Store" or the "App Store and Identified Developers."

Keychain Access Password Manager

To ensure the safety of your online presence, it is essential to protect your accounts by using passwords that are difficult to guess. The management of a large number of passwords, on the other hand, can be difficult, particularly when the passwords differ between various accounts. In situations like this, the Keychain Access software shows to be really useful.

You may save all of your passwords in a secure location with Keychain Access, which also provides convenient access whenever it is needed. Moreover, it keeps track of the dates on which your passwords expire, ensuring that you are always up to date.

Keychain Access ensures a high level of security by employing the most highly advanced encryption methods currently available. Every single file in the keychain is encrypted using a one-of-a-kind key that is exclusive to your device. In light of this, even if the keychain file were to become compromised, it would still be necessary to have knowledge of the encryption key for your computer in order to access your passwords.

Keychain Access is the answer for Mac users who are looking for a solution that is both effective and efficient for managing their passwords. Just follow these steps in order to gain access to it:

- Enter the name of the Utility folder that is contained within the Applications folder.
- To launch the application, double-click the Keychain Access icon.
- After agreeing to a browser' save password' offer, you will be presented with a number of keychains upon launch. One of these keychains is the Login keychain, which is where passwords for a variety of websites are collected and kept.
- In addition, you have the option of storing your Keychain in a safe online location using iCloud, which enables you to access it from

different devices, such as iPhones, iPads, and other Macs.

Mail Privacy Protection

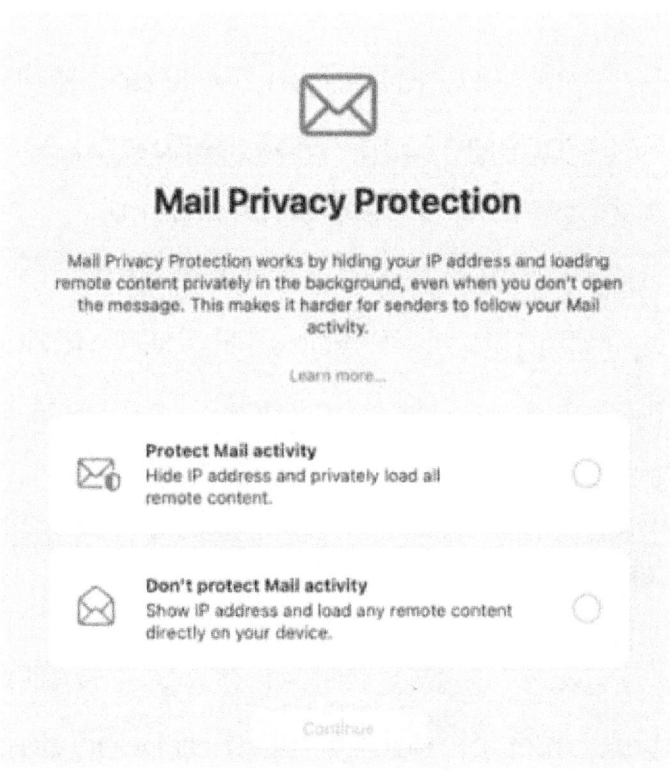

MacBook Air M3, the latest version of macOS, includes a brand new feature called Mail Privacy Protection. It provides users with protection against email senders who are seeking to monitor email opens or obtain location information from their IP addresses.

Proceed with the following steps in order to determine whether or not this feature is active on your Mac:

- On your Mac, launch the **Mail application**.
- After that, go to the **Mail menu** and choose it.
- Also, go to the **Preferences menu.**
- Ensure that "Protect Mail Activity" is enabled by going to the Privacy tab and making sure that it is enabled (it should be enabled by default).

Find My Mac

Find My Mac is the last and most well-known security feature of macOS that has been discussed in this collection. The Find My Mac application, which was developed particularly for the purpose of preventing theft of Macs, gives customers the ability to pinpoint the position of their computer, lock it remotely, and delete all of its data if it becomes essential to do so.

If you want to set up Find My Mac, here is how:

- Enter the **System Preferences menu.**
- You can choose between **Internet Accounts or Apple ID**.
- From the available options, select **iCloud.**
- The **Find My Mac box** should be checked, and access should be granted.

After the configuration is complete, you will be able to track the location of your MacBook Air M3 device by using either iCloud.com or the Find My iPhone app on another iOS device.

CHAPTER SIXTEEN

Tips and tricks

If you have just recently purchased your first Mac, there are a few crucial steps that you need to perform in order to guarantee that your experience with your new computer becomes as easy and joyful as possible.

There is a growing group of people who are making their first steps toward owning a Mac, whether it is because of the generous presents they received from loved ones or because they took advantage of the chance presented by enticing discounts.

It is highly likely that you are a member of this fascinating group of people who are beginning their journey with a Mac if you are reading this. You are very welcome! You are at the very beginning of your journey, and your MacBook Air M3 device is still securely packaged inside its manufacturer's packaging.

In addition to merely unpacking everything, the following are some vital activities that you will want to carry out with your brand-new computing device.

As you prepare your new Mac, here are twenty important steps to take into consideration.

Things you should know about your new device

1. Familiarize yourself with your ports and connect your devices accordingly.

The physical layout of your MacBook Air M3 devices is not something that everyone is aware with, despite the fact that it can appear to be common knowledge. The process of unboxing provides the ideal time to become acquainted with your device before settling it into its principal place.

A moment of your time is required to locate the ports, with reference to the documentation that is included. Port selection mirrors the sleekness of the laptop itself. Positioned on the left side are a pair of Thunderbolt 4/USB-C ports, while a headphone jack graces the right. Additionally, a MagSafe charging port is available, although the laptop can also be charged using the USB-C ports for added flexibility.

Generally speaking, Apple uses connectors that are commonly used and that you are probably already aware with. Some examples of these ports include HDMI for video, USB-A, and USB-C. It should be brought to your attention that USB-C ports are also capable of supporting Thunderbolt connections, which expands their utility beyond the capabilities of ordinary USB ports.

MagSafe, which provides a dedicated power port, has been reintroduced in the most recent MacBook Air models, which are 13 and 15 inches in size.

You will be able to identify what devices you are able to connect to your Mac and how to effectively manage wires in your workspace if you take a moment to evaluate the ports that are available to you. Furthermore, it may inspire you to consider making an investment in an additional dock in order to broaden the range of ports that you can choose from.

2. **Setting up your MacBook**

Even though this may at first appear to be a daunting task, keep in mind that it is a one-time process that will continue until you purchase a new Mac. You will be able to navigate through each step with the assistance of Apple, which has made the process quite simple.

Although it is possible to treat all the components at once, there is typically the option to proceed without addressing specific components. There is the possibility of completing or modifying any sections that were skipped at a later time.

Begin by turning on the Mac, selecting your nation or region, and activating any accessibility options that may be required. Following this, you will need to establish your connection to the network, which may require you to enter a password for the Wi-Fi hotspot.

When you have successfully established access to the network and the internet, you will be invited to determine whether or not you wish to move data to your new Mac. This process can be made easier with the assistance of the Migration Assistant, even if you are moving from a Windows desktop application. On the other hand, delaying this step and carrying it out at a later time is not prohibited in any way.

Using the Migration Assistant, the process of transferring data to your new Mac is simplified.

3. Creating an Apple ID for yourself

If this is your first time purchasing a Mac, there is a good possibility that you are already accustomed with controlling an iPhone or iPad. Your Apple ID and password are required to access your Mac, just like they are for those other devices. You have the option of establishing a connection to iCloud on your Mac either with the Apple ID system setting after the initial setup process has been completed or during the process itself. If you skipped this step during the initial setup process, I strongly advise you to finish it as soon as possible in order to guarantee the safety of your data through iCloud and to ensure that it is synchronized.

You may eliminate the need for physical tethering or manual synchronization by integrating iCloud across all of your devices. This will allow you to share photographs, contacts, calendars, and other information in a seamless manner.

Keychain, which keeps your passwords and sensitive data in a secure manner, and Find My, which helps you to locate and manage your lost or stolen Mac, are two of the main services that require an active Apple ID. There are several more functions that require an active Apple ID. If you have not yet established an Apple ID, this moment presents you with the ideal opportunity to do so.

4. Backup with Time Machine

The use of Time Machine to create a backup of your Mac is absolutely necessary in order to protect your valuable data and to ensure that you have peace of mind with your new Mac configuration. Despite the fact that some people could miss this step, putting together a fundamental backup plan is not only simple but also cost-effective.

Before you can get started, you will need an external drive. A standard external hard drive that connects by USB-A or USB-C will be sufficient, even though that a network-attached storage device is an option. There are tools available from third-party developers; however, making use of the Time Machine feature that is integrated into the software offers sufficient security. Find the icon that looks like a clock with a counterclockwise arrow in the menu bar, click on it, and then pick "Open Time Machine Preferences." This will start the procedure. Optionally, you can access Time Machine by clicking on the **Apple icon** located in the upper-left corner of the menu bar. After that, you can go to **System Preferences** and choose **Time Machine** from the list of options.

After you have successfully connected your external drive to the Mac, pick "Select Backup Disk," then select the drive you want to use, and finally select "Use Disk." You may want to consider selecting "Encrypt Backups" if you want to increase your level of privacy.

Time Machine will automatically back up your files or any changes you make to them every hour while your Mac is active and attached to the drive. This will happen after the initial setup has been completed. In spite of the fact that the initial backup could take some time, repeated backups guarantee that your data is protected from being lost by accident.

Consider purchasing AppleCare+ as an additional measure of protection against the possibility of experiencing hardware problems. This could potentially save you from having to pay expensive repair expenses.

5. Get familiar with the System Preferences.

It is highly likely that **System Preferences** will be the tool that you will turn to if you intend to make significant adjustments to the settings on your Mac. If you want to access the interface that is comparable to the Control Panel in Windows, all you have to do is click the **Apple icon** in the menu bar, and then select **System Preferences.**

System Preferences comprises a variety of areas, such as the management of your Apple ID, preferences for the display, alterations to the functionality of macOS, network settings, and controls for peripherals and features.

It is possible that you will come across situations in which the settings are initially locked and cannot be modified. This is done for reasons of security. Authenticate yourself by entering your account password after you have located the padlock icon in the bottom left corner of the window. This will allow you to unlock them. When you have finished making the necessary adjustments, it is recommended that you re-lock the settings by clicking the open padlock once more. This will ensure that they continue to be secure.

6. Multi-Touch Gestures on Your Mac

It is possible that you are not familiar with the variety of Multi-Touch gestures that are available to quickly carry out a variety of actions if you are new to the Mac family.

It is important to make the most of these gestures because Apple has painstakingly designed them to be easy to understand and simple to remember. One or more fingers can be used to do a variety of functions when using a Multi-Touch trackpad or Magic Mouse. These devices allow you to tap, swipe, squeeze, or spread your fingers.

For instance, you can activate the Notification Center by swiping left from the right side of the screen with two fingers, or you can tap with three fingers to look up a word in the dictionary in order to access the dictionary.

To gain a more in-depth understanding of these motions, go to the **System Preferences menu** before selecting either the Trackpad or the Mouse. In this section, you will be able to disable gestures, adjust their functionality, and find out whether gestures are compatible with your Mac.

7. Identifying the Screen Size That Is Most Appropriate for You

You might have to go through a process of trial and error in order to get the ideal screen size. Although macOS provides a default option for scaling the screen, it is possible that not everyone may find it to be satisfactory. Select **Displays** from the menu that appears after you click on **the Apple icon** located in the upper left corner of your screen to access **System Preferences**. This will allow you to investigate many alternative alternatives.

Once you are there, select **Scaled** from the **Resolution menu.** This provides you with the ability to personalize your display, allowing you to choose whether you want larger text or more screen real estate. Try out a variety of various configurations to determine which one works best for you. At the moment, I am entirely pleased with the Default configuration; but, the possibilities that **More Space** presents are very intriguing to me.

In addition to that, there are two extra settings that I always make sure to disable. Considering that I place a high importance on having full control over my screen experience, I have disabled the option to "Automatically adjust brightness." My preference is to manually control the brightness of my screen rather than letting macOS to make adjustments based on the light conditions in the surrounding environment.

Similar to how I choose not to use True Tone, an Apple function that automatically adjusts display colors based on the illumination in the surrounding environment, I do not use True Tone. I find that it frequently adjusts colors in a manner that does not line with my choices, particularly when I am working on picture and video editing activities on my MacBook Air M3 device. Although it is intended to offer proper white balance, I frequently find that it does not follow my preferences.

8. Become familiar with the Apple menu

The Apple Menu, which can be found in the upper left corner of the screen of your Mac, provides you with easy access to a variety of other functions. When you click on it, you will have instant access to the system preferences of your Mac, the Mac App Store, as well as information about recently opened applications and documents. Additionally, you can restart or shut down your Mac by using the Apple Menu by selecting the appropriate option.

The Apple Menu includes a function that is particularly helpful especially if an application suddenly stops responding due to a fault. This tool is called **Force Quit.** Within a short amount of time, this feature will kill an application that is causing you problems, allowing you to restart your computer and immediately resume your work.

9. Exploring Menu Bar

One of the most important aspects of the graphical user experience is the menu bar, which is a visual interface element that houses dropdown menus. This application is designed to consolidate application-specific menus and is specifically optimized for Mac computers.

Unlike Windows and a large number of Linux desktop environments, macOS takes a different approach to desktop administration. Instead of assigning each application its own menu, it uses a single, global menu bar that dynamically adjusts itself to the application that is now being used. When it comes to the user interface, macOS is defined by its consistency and continuity.

A basic app launcher, status menus, and easy access to the Control Center and notifications are some of the extra features that are integrated into the macOS menu bar in addition to its primary role. Customizability is a noteworthy feature that gives users the option to personalize both the design and the operation of the product to suit their tastes.

An intuitive and ever-present interface is provided by the macOS menu bar, which is comprised of a system menu, a persistent app menu, and a suite of status icons. Because of its pervasiveness, it facilitates familiarity and simplicity of navigation, which makes it an essential component of the Mac experience.

10.   Customizing the Dock's

The panel of icons that may be found at the bottom of the screen of your Mac is known as the Dock. New Macs such as the MacBook Air M3 come with Apple's own built-in applications, such as Safari, Mail, Contacts, Calendars, and Notes, preloaded into the Dock by default. These applications are built into the Mac. On the other hand, you are allowed to modify it in accordance with your individual preferences.

When you customize your Dock, you have the ability to display only the applications that are relevant to you. To streamline the appearance of the Dock, simply drag some applications, such as Maps or FaceTime, out of the Dock until the word "Remove" appears. This will streamline the appearance of the Dock. In contrast, if you use Mail regularly, you might want to try shifting it to the left side of the screen for better access. Additionally, you may add applications, directories, and files that you use regularly by dragging and dropping them into the Dock. This is a very straightforward process.

The size can also be changed, the "Open" signs can be removed, the bouncing animation can be turned off, and there are further customization options. Given that your Dock is an essential component of your Desktop, you should make sure to devote sufficient time to personalizing it to your precise tastes.

11.   Launchpad and the Mac App Store

Launchpad, which is an icon that can be found in the Dock positioned at the bottom of your screen, makes it easy to access the majority of the software that is installed on your Mac. To open Launchpad, you can either click on its icon or use a pinch gesture with your thumb and three fingers. Both of these methods are available to you. Upon selection, a panel that fills the entire screen will appear, displaying the applications that have been installed and are ready for immediate use.

Investigating the Mac App Store is yet another alternative, despite the fact that it is possible to obtain extra applications directly from the worldwide web. A broad variety of applications may be downloaded and installed into your Mac through the Mac App Store, which is comparable to its counterpart for the iPhone and iPad. All of this can be done with a minimum of hassle.

In addition, the Mac App Store simplifies the process of updating applications by providing you with timely notifications whenever more updates are made available for installation.

12.   Explore Preinstalled Apps

If you purchase a Mac for the first time, you will discover that macOS already has a number of applications pre-installed and ready for you to use. These apps are designed to meet a variety of requirements, including those pertaining to creativity, education, productivity, and amusement.

Take, for example, the applications Numbers, Pages, and Keynote, which are Apple's equivalents of Microsoft Excel, Word, and PowerPoint, respectively. You will also find the Mail app, which allows you to manage your email, and the Calendar app, which allows you to organize your schedule. However, you will be need to set up both of these apps first in order for them to sync with your existing online accounts.

Those who are interested in photography can make use of the Photos app, while those who are passionate about music will like the Audio app that is already included. Composing music and editing videos are two of the creative undertakings that may be accomplished with the help of GarageBand and iMovie.

Because these applications come pre-installed, users do not have to go to the Mac App Store in order to use the vast array of features that are easily available. Spend some time investigating them and learning about the possibilities they provide.

13.   Modifying the Trackpad Settings

A wide variety of options and configurations are available for the Trackpad, which enables the user to have a very personalized experience. If you are experienced with using a Mac, it is possible that you already have plans for the settings that you prefer to use. My personal preference is to disable the tap-to-click capability as well as the single-finger force click for the purpose of looking up something and clicking. In order to have access to these configurations, go to **System Preferences** and then select **Trackpad.**

You have the ability to fine-tune a variety of variables included inside the Trackpad settings. You have the ability to modify the tapping options beneath the "Point and Click" section. Under the heading "Scroll and Zoom," you have the ability to adjust the behavior of scrolling, and under the heading "More Gestures," you have the ability to personalize more options.

By switching the Natural scrolling option off in the "Scroll and Zoom" tab, which changes the direction in which scrolling occurs, many users choose to manually modify the scrolling direction.

14. Ensure you download the appropriate version of apps

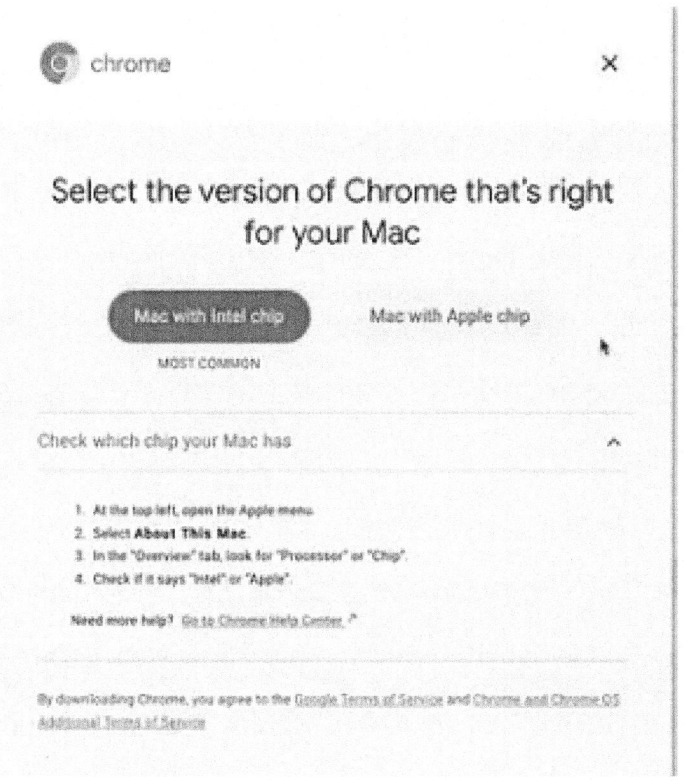

Depending on the processor that your computer is equipped with, several developers offer a variety of various versions of their applications. As an illustration, when you download Chrome from a website rather than the Mac App Store, Google will ask you to specify whether you have an Intel or

Mac M3 device. If you are unsure, you will be provided with steps to validate your identification.

15.   Window Management and Force Quit

When the number of windows on your screen begins to increase, it is imperative that you acquire the skills necessary to successfully manage them. Three dots are often located in the upper-left area of the screen, which is where the principal controls are located.

The current window is closed by the dot on the leftmost side of the window, which is often red and has a smaller dot in the middle. You can minimize the window to the Dock by clicking the central dot, which is often yellow with a dash symbol.

The options for basic window management are represented by these three dots.

The application is able to enter full-screen mode when the rightmost dot, which appears green and displays a + symbol when the mouse is moved over it, is clicked within the application. When you mouse over certain applications, you may be presented with extra options. These options may include the ability to zoom into the application, shift it to the left or right half of the display, or relocate it to another connected screen if you have more than one display.

Double-tapping the title bar of the window allows you to switch between full-screen and original sizes of the window.

You may adjust the size of the majority of windows by clicking and dragging the cursor over their sides, bottoms, or corners, and then dragging the cursor.

Let us assume that an application stops responding and displays the "spinning beachball," the initial step is to make an attempt to close the window in the same manner as before. Also, if it is required, end the application in the appropriate manner by right-clicking its icon in the macOS Dock and selecting "Quit."

It is recommended that you make use of the Force Quit option, which can be accessed through the Apple icon located in the menu bar, if these instructions are unsuccessful. It is recommended that this effort be made before resorting to restarting the device.

16.   Set up the Night Shift

During the nighttime hours, the display colors of your brand-new MacBook Air M3 will automatically adapt themselves to generate warmer tones. This feature is included in the device. Using a laptop in low-light situations is made easier by this feature, which reduces the quantity of blue light that is emitted. Additionally, this feature encourages better sleep after using the laptop. Nevertheless, in order to make use of this capacity, you will need to activate it.

The way to accomplish this is to go to **System Preferences**, then **Display**s, then **Night Shift**, and finally **Schedule.**

Through this menu, you have the option of selecting automatic activation from sunset to morning, or you can create a timetable that is tailored to your specific needs. You also have the ability to fine-tune the temperature adjustment to fit your preferences, which is a considerable amount of freedom.

17.　　Unlock the Full Potential of Dictation

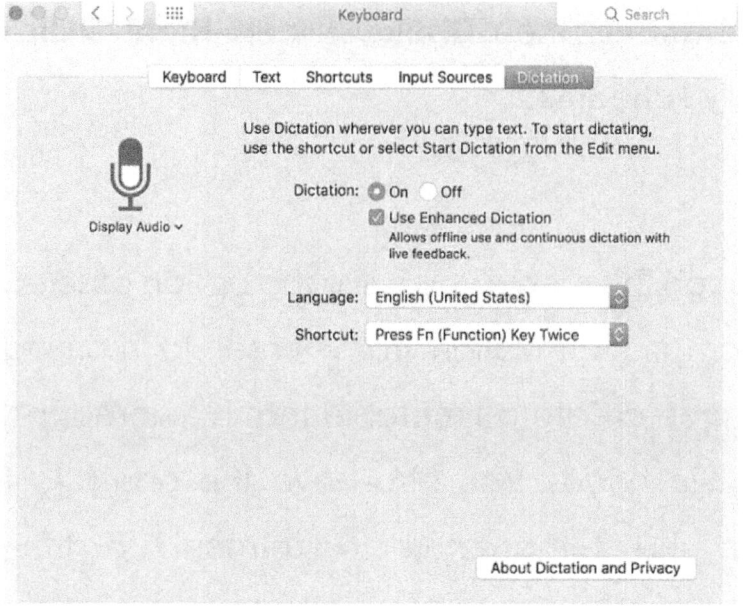

Apple's Dictation is a powerful speech-to-text solution that provides a convenient way to swiftly jot down notes or compose messages without having to use your hands. Dictation functions in a manner that is consistent across all platforms, regardless of whether you are using an iPhone or a Mac. To begin, you need only press the button that activates the microphone, start speaking, and then observe how your words readily materialize in the text box.

On more recent Macs like the MacBook Air M3, the button that controls the microphone is conveniently situated on the keyboard as the F5 key. You may also enable dictation by going to the "Edit" option in the Menu Bar and selecting "Start Dictation." This is an alternative method. Accessing "System Preferences" > "Keyboard" > "Dictation" is still another way that may be used to personalize the keyboard shortcut that you wish to use for activation.

18.   Activating "Do Not Disturb"

The interruptions that occur when you are concentrating on a task can be very disturbing. It is recommended that you try setting the "Do Not Disturb" function on your Mac in order to silence notifications in order to retain your productivity.

In this manner:

- Simply go to the **System Preferences menu** and select **Notifications.**

- Configure the "Do Not Disturb" option inside Notifications so that it will activate automatically at certain times, such as when the display is sleeping, when the screen is locked, or when you are mirroring to a television or projector.

19.   Using Spotlight to Conduct Searches in an Effective Manner

Once you have Siri activated, you have already accessed a powerful tool that can assist you in locating the information that you require within macOS.

Within macOS, Spotlight functions as a search engine that can be used by either selecting the magnifying glass icon located in the menu bar or by using the keyboard shortcut Command-Space. This will bring up a text bar where you may immediately begin putting in your inquiry once it is displayed.

In addition to looking for text and filenames on your Mac, Spotlight is also capable of handling a wide variety of other search topics. This encompasses the locations on Maps, the inquiries made on the internet, and the fundamental unit conversions.

For additional convenience, you can quickly access particular system options, such as the Do Not Disturb option, just by searching for them. In order to open an application more quickly, it is more efficient to use the keyboard shortcut and type out the name of the application rather than using the mouse or trackpad to click on its icon. This is a power-user move that can be accomplished by learning how to use Spotlight properly.

20.　　Ensuring that your Mac is up to date

Last but not least, it is of the utmost importance to verify that the operating system of your new Mac is up to date. If you update your Mac to the most recent version of macOS, you will have access to the most recent features and changes that have been made to improve its performance and usability.

This is the next step to take:

- From the Apple menu, which is located in the upper-left corner of the screen, pick "About This Mac."
- In the subsequent step, select the "Software Update" button that appears in the pop-up window.
- The next step is for your Mac to check for any available updates.
- This will be confirmed by the pop-up if your Mac is already running the most recent version. In that case, you will be presented

with the available update. Clicking the "**Upgrade Now**" button will start the process of updating the software.

CHAPTER SEVENTEEN

Troubleshooting

Do you find that your MacBook Air M3 is giving you trouble? Errors occasionally manifest themselves, regardless of whether you are making use of an older model or the most recent generation. This chapter is intended to provide you with assistance in resolving issues in a timely manner.

If you want to discover the solution you need as quickly as possible, you should look through the following list of frequent problems that Air users experience.

Common problems you might encounter with your new device

1. The MacBook Air M3 is unable to turn on.

Solution;

- **Check the current status of the screen:** Try to determine whether the MacBook is turned off or whether the screen is the only component that is not functioning properly. Take note of whether the Caps Lock key illuminates, whether hitting the power button causes a chiming sound to be produced, and whether the keyboard has a tiny warmth to it. However, if the answer is yes, the problem most likely resides with the screen. The next step in the troubleshooting process is to proceed.
- **Look into the power supply:** Check to see that the MacBook is not simply having power

issues. Determine whether the battery has been charged to the appropriate level and whether the laptop may be used when it is connected to a power source. If at all feasible, do the test using a different power cord. If you are unable to power on, there could be a problem with the battery or the power cord. When you want to isolate potential conflicts, you should disconnect peripherals like the mouse and mobile devices.

- **Carry out a completely restart:** Depress and maintain pressure on the Power button for a minimum of ten seconds. In order to determine whether or not the MacBook is powered on, press the Power button once more.

- **Do away with the manual upgrades:** On extremely rare occasions, the MacBook may become inoperable due to the installation of manual upgrades such as more memory. Despite the fact that MacBook Air M3 models are not normally upgradeable by the user, it is important to undo any alterations, whether they are internal or external, in order to adequately troubleshoot the issue.

2. The screen is not functioning properly.

The solution is as follows:

- **Perform a hard reset:** It is recommended that you perform a hard restart if your laptop is functioning properly but the screen continues to act sluggish. After pressing and holding the Power button for a minimum of ten seconds, you should press it once more to determine whether or not the screen turns on.

- **Update your device:** Always make sure that the software on your MacBook is up to date. If you are experiencing problems with an external display, you should update your MacBook. Make that the cable is still attached, and then use the Dock to access the System Preferences menu. On the off chance that your system is out of date, select **Software Update** and install any available updates for the Mac operating system, firmware, or other relevant tasks.

- **Make use of Apple Adapters:** Apple adapters should be used because there is a possibility that third-party second screen adapters will cause compatibility issues with the MacBook Air M3 models. For uninterrupted connectivity, make sure you are using adapters that have been approved by Apple.

- **Reach out to Apple Support:** If your MacBook Air M3 models show indicators of being powered on (such as sounds and lights), but the screen remains entirely dark and there is no movement of the pointer, it is possible that you will need to contact Apple Support in order to successfully repair the issue.

3. The battery on my MacBook Air M3 model does not charge

Solution;

- **Verify Adapter compatibility:** In order to ensure that you are using the appropriate adapter and charging cable, it is important to check that the adapter is compatible. It is important to keep in mind that both L-style and T-style adapters are compatible with the same computer if you purchase a MagSafe charger. The MagSafe 2 connectors, on the other hand, are not compatible with those PCs. For compatibility purposes, an additional adapter is necessary in order to use L or T adapters with MagSafe 2 ports that are compatible. In order to differentiate between the many types of connectors, refer to Apple's visual reference.

- **Be on the lookout for any evidence of damage**: Inspect the adapter cable as well as the ports on your MacBook Air M3 for any indications of damaged components. If you are making use of the correct cable with the correct model of MacBook Air M3, you need to make sure that neither the cable nor the port has any physical impairments.

- **Change Electrical Outlet**: In order to change the electrical outlet, first disconnect the adapter from the power outlet for a period of approximately one minute, and then reconnect it. The presence of line noise on the circuit may be indicated if the charging process is able to resume after this interruption. If you want to troubleshoot the problem, you might want to think about charging the MacBook Air M3 using a new electrical circuit or unplugging other appliances from the circuit that is currently being used.

4. **Rapid discharge of the battery**

Solutions;

- **Upgrade Your Mac**: Select **Software Update** from the **System Preferences menu** that appears when you open the Dock. If there are any updates available, you should install them. In order to restart your Mac when the installation is complete, click the **Apple icon** located in the menu bar and then select the **Restart option**. Also, check to see if this fixes the problem.

- **Verify the Application's energy consumption:** If you want to see which applications are using a substantial amount of energy, click on the **Battery symbol.** Find any applications that are routinely consuming a lot of energy and close them to see if this causes the battery life to increase.

- **Reset SMC (Non-T2 Security Chip):** There are situations when resetting the SMC can be of assistance. Click the **Apple icon** located in the menu bar, and then select the Shut Down option to bring your Mac to a complete shutdown. After it has been turned off, press and hold the **Shift key**, the **Control key**, and the **Option key** simultaneously for ten seconds while also pressing and holding the **Power button**. When you are ready to power on your Mac, let go of all the keys and then push the **Power button**.

- **Reset SMC (T2 Security Chip):** You may reset the SMC (T2 Security Chip) by turning off your Mac by selecting the **Shut Down option** from the Apple menu. Before reconnecting the power cord to the wall outlet, first unhook it from the outlet and wait fifteen seconds before doing so. After you have successfully reconnected, you should wait an extra five seconds before turning on your Mac once more.

5. A problem with the MacBook Air M3 overheating

Solutions:

- **Investigate running applications:** The Activity Monitor can be accessed by first clicking on "Go" in the menu bar, then selecting "Utilities," and finally beginning the process of opening "Activity Monitor." You can determine which applications are taking a considerable amount of CPU time and energy by checking the CPU tab. When you find any applications that are foreign to you or that require a lot of resources, you can terminate them by selecting their name and clicking on the "Stop" icon that is placed in the top-left corner of the screen (it looks like a "X" inside of an octagon).

- **Inspect the fan:** It is important to check the fan since an overheated environment can be caused by a fan that is not functioning properly. Ascertain whether or not the fan is functioning by listening for any sounds that are not typical. Let's assume that there is no audible noise, it is possible that it is still operating at a slower speed. If, on the other hand, you are performing activities that generally require a significant amount of CPU usage, such as playing a difficult game through Steam, and the fan is not making any noise, you might want to consider running diagnostics or getting in touch with Apple for assistance.

- **Clear the vent:** It is important to clean the vent because the collection of debris in the vent that is placed at the back hinge area can prevent the proper dissipation of heat. On a regular basis, use a can of compressed air to remove any dust or particles that have gathered or accumulated.

- **Run Apple Diagnostics**: After turning off the MacBook entirely, disconnect all the devices that are connected to it. To begin the Apple Diagnostics check, hit the **Power button,** and then immediately press and hold **the D key** until the check begins. After following the instructions that appear on the screen, make a note of the error codes and instructions that are supplied in the event that any errors are found. After the diagnostics have been finished, restart the MacBook.

- **Take off the third-party case or shell:** Although third-party cases and shells frequently include vents that allow for the dispersion of heat, the quality of these accessories might vary. In order to determine whether or not the case helps reduce the overheating issue, briefly remove it. If deleting the case causes the issue to be resolved, you might think about replacing it with an option of greater quality.

6. Unable to hear any sound on the MacBook Air M3

Solutions:

Upgrade Your Mac:

- Access **Software Update** by navigating to System Preferences on the Dock and selecting it.
- If your Mac is not up to date, install any updates that are available.
- After you have finished updating, you will need to restart your Mac by selecting Restart from the menu bar after clicking the Apple icon. Verify that the sound problem continues to exist.

Reset PRAM/NVRAM:

- Proceed to the menu bar, click the **Apple logo,** and then select **the Shut Down option.**
- In order to turn on your Mac, press the **Power button** and then immediately press and hold

the Command, Option, P, and R keys simultaneously before turning it on.

- Hold down the keys for around twenty seconds; it is possible that your Mac will restart during this procedure.

- You should let off of the keys when you hear the startup chime for the second time when the Apple logo disappears for the second time.

- By performing this operation, all modified login settings that could potentially affect sound setups will be reversed.

A visit to an Apple Store or an Authorized Service Provider is recommended.

- It is advised that units manufactured from the beginning of 2010 go with this choice.

- It is possible for technicians working at Apple Stores or Authorized Service Providers to diagnose and repair certain hardware-related issues; however, the process may include expensive replacements.

7. The trackpad is not operating properly:

Solutions:

- **Clean and dry the trackpad**: It is important to clean and dry the trackpad since moisture, filth, and dust can interfere with the performance of the trackpad, which can result in abnormal behavior such as the pointer leaping or the trackpad not responding. Before beginning the cleaning process, remember to turn off the Mac.

- **Reset the PRAM:** You can refer to the instructions that were provided before in order to execute a PRAM reset and determine whether or not this resolves the issue.

- **Run Apple Diagnostics:** Completely power down the Mac, and disconnect any devices that are secondary to it. While simultaneously pressing the **Power button**, immediately press and hold the **D key** until Apple Diagnostics begins to run. To perform the diagnostic check, follow the instructions that appear on the screen. It is important to take note of the error codes and advice that are offered in the report if any issues are found. After you have finished the diagnostic process, you can return to MacOS by clicking the **Restart button.**

8. Application Freeze

Solutions:

- **Restart the application:** If the application is not responding, choose "Force Quit" from the context menu that appears when you right-click on the application. This will force the application to close. If you are only able to select the "Quit" option, you will need to press and hold the **Option key** until the options change to "Force Quit." Then, in order to fix the problem, you should try restarting the application.

- **Verify that there are any updates:** To access the "Updates" area of the App Store, open it from the Dock and then head over to the left side of the screen. Download and install any updates that are available for the application.

- **Perform a complete system shutdown:** If the entire system is frozen, you should consider initiating a forced shutdown. Additionally, you should do a complete shutdown of the system. While holding down the Power button, press and hold it for approximately ten seconds until the system automatically turns off.

- **Await a patch:** It is possible that the application will not be compatible with the most recent version of macOS if you have just updated your operating system. From the perspective of the application developer, this calls for an update to be implemented.

Ensure that you are aware of any patches or updates that may be provided by the developer.

9. Not Able to Make Use of AirPrint

Solutions:

- **Be sure to check for updates**: Using AirPrint might be difficult because it relies on third-party devices, which may not always synchronize without any problems. Go to the App Store on the Dock, and then pick "Updates" from the left panel of the menu that appears. Continue with the installation of any updates that are linked with the application.

- **Update Printer Firmware:** In order to update the firmware on your printer, you need search the internet for your particular printer model, preferably on the official website of the manufacturer. All notifications and firmware upgrades that pertain to AirPrint compatibility will be accessible through that location if they are available. You should download and install any updates that are required. However, it is important to keep in mind that even while some printers have wireless capabilities, not all printers are compatible with AirPrint.

- **Confirm Connection:** It is necessary for printers to establish a direct wireless connection to AirPrint in order to confirm the connection. In the case of AirPrint compatibility, for example, simply being connected to an AirPort device is not sufficient to ensure compatibility.

- **Reboot Everything:** Despite the fact that it is uncomfortable, restarting everything is frequently the only option available if no other remedy is successful. The router, the printer, and the MacBook should all be turned off and then turned back on in the order that they were previously turned off. It is sometimes necessary to do a hard reboot in order to resolve any underlying problems.

10.   Malfunctioning USB port:

Solutions;

- **Diagnose hardware functionality:** To determine if the issue is with the port or the device itself, it is necessary to test other USB devices in order to diagnose the functionality of the hardware. To discover whether the problem is particular to one USB port or whether it affects all of them, you should try to establish a connection using different USB ports. There is a possibility that a single port is physically broken if it is causing problems. Determine whether there are any indications of bending, looseness, or other physical anomalies. You should seek assistance at an Apple Store if you feel that the port has been damaged. Let's also assume all ports are experiencing problems (although the USB device is operating normally), you should restart your Mac and check for any available system upgrades.

- **SMC reset:** To do an SMC reset, go to the menu bar and select the **Apple logo.** Then, select the **Shut Down option.** Immediately after the device has been turned off, simultaneously press and hold the Shift, Control, and Option keys together with the **Power button** for ten seconds, and then let go of the devices. After then, you should push the Power button more than once.

11. My MacBook Air is unresponsive when attempting to shut down.

Solutions:

- **Check for unfinished business:** If you are attempting to power down your MacBook Air M3 device and it continues to be active without showing any signs of turning off, you should wait between five and ten minutes to be sure that it is not currently working on any tasks that are still active. Before beginning the process of shutting down the computer, it is important to check the Mac operating system for any pending alarms, notifications, or running apps that could require attention. It is important to pay attention to tiny indications such as program icons in the Dock that are jumping, as they could be signs of activities running in the background.

- **Dealing with frozen applications**: If the MacBook Air M3 is unable to shut down because of a frozen application, right-click on the icon of the application in question and select "Force Quit" to end the application's function. In the event that the "Force Quit" option does not show, you can force it to appear by pressing and holding the **Option key** while right-clicking on the icon of the application.

- **Force a complete shutdown:** Also, if the MacBook Air M3 device continues to be unresponsive despite your efforts to end applications, you can force a complete shutdown by holding down the **Power button** for a minimum of ten seconds. This will result in the device being powered off entirely. But you should proceed with caution because this method has the potential to disrupt ongoing system updates. Before carrying out a forced shutdown, check to see that there are no applications or updates that are still waiting to be installed.

12.   Issues with the Connectivity of Wi-Fi

Solutions:

- **Restart the Wi-Fi:** To begin, turn the Wi-Fi off and then turn it back on. Click the Wi-Fi icon that is placed on the menu bar, then move the Wi-Fi switch to the off position, wait a time, and then move it back to the on position. When you take this one operation, you will frequently reestablish a connection to the local network and regain access to the internet.

- **Perform a Complete Restart**: When dealing with Wi-Fi troubles, it is necessary to perform a complete reset because these issues can be rather complicated. Beginning with the modem, proceed to switch off the router, and then turn off the Mac. When you have finished pausing for a moment, turn them back on in the same order. By carrying out this method, any potential hurdles that may be preventing connectivity between these devices are effectively removed.

- **Update macOS:** Maintaining an up-to-date version of your operating system, macOS, can help you fix issues with your wireless network. Software Update may be accessed by navigating to **System Preferences** on the Dock and selecting it. It is recommended that you proceed with the installation of any available updates in order to potentially restore Wi-Fi capability.

- **Take Advantage of the 5GHz Band**: If it is possible, you should think about connecting to the 5GHz band. The 5GHz frequency is often less congested than the other bands, which might help alleviate connectivity concerns despite the fact that it has a shorter range. You can switch to this band by going to the menu bar and selecting the Wi-Fi symbol. From there, choose the 5GHz connection that is appropriate. It is important to keep in mind that this technique necessitates the 5GHz band having its own SSID, which may not be accessible on routers and kits that automatically balance devices by use a single SSID.

13.   **FaceTime is not operating as it should be being used**.

Solutions;

- **Camera Check:** Make sure that the lens of the camera is clear of any obstructions by doing a camera check. Taking off any objects that are covering the camera and could potentially hinder its functionality, such as black tape or other materials, is quite important.

- **FaceTime Settings Verification**: In order to verify your FaceTime settings, launch the FaceTime application and go to the **Preferences section** of the corresponding menu bar. First, check to see if FaceTime is validated or if it displays the message "waiting for activation." Following the procedures to validate FaceTime through your email is what you need to do if it is in the latter condition.

- **Check the Fundamental Information**: Make sure that your phone number, location, and any other pertinent facts are correctly configured by going to the Preferences menu and checking them twice.

- **Update and restart:** From the Dock, navigate to **System Preferences** and pick **Software Update** from the menu that appears. The next step is to restart your device from the same menu once you have installed any updates that are currently available.

- **Get in touch with Apple Support:** If the problem continues to occur despite the measures described above, it may be an indication that there is a hardware issue with the camera. In situations like these, you should contact Apple Support in order to receive additional support and advice on how to resolve the issue.

14. **Experiencing Frequent User Interface Lag**

Solution:

- **Restart your Mac:** If you are experiencing user interface slowness on your MacBook Air M3 device, such as choppy animations and visuals when opening applications or resizing windows, restarting your Mac can frequently remedy the issue. To restart, simply select the Restart option from the menu bar by clicking on the **Apple logo.**

- **Verify that there are any updates:** By selecting **Software Update** from the **System Preferences** menu that appears in the Dock, you can make sure that your computer is running the most recent version. Install any updates that are available if they are required.

- **Restore your Mac by doing the following:** It is possible that driver corruption is the cause of the UI slowness if updating macOS does not address the issue. In circumstances like these, reinstalling macOS from the macOS Recovery program can be the remedy that is required.

15. Applications constantly crashing

Solutions:

- **Verify that there are any updates:** Launch the **App Store** from the Dock, and then select the **Updates tab** located on the left side of the screen. Put in place any updates that are available for the app that is giving you trouble.

- **Simply remove and then reinstall:** Launch the **Finder application** from the Dock, and then open the **Applications menu** from the sidebar. Find the application that is causing the issue, and either drag it to the trash or utilize the "Move to trash" option that is in the File menu. Try reinstalling the application to see if the problem still occurs.

- **Deal with issues related to overheating:** Once you have used your device for an extended period of time, if it seems excessively hot, it may be overheating. In order to allow your laptop to cool down for around thirty minutes, you should reduce the amount of applications that are running simultaneously and power it down.

CONCLUSION

The MacBook Air M3 stands out as a top choice among laptops, particularly catering to a specific demographic: the work-casual user. In this niche, it excels, offering a combination of lightweight design, impressive power, comfortable typing experience, and unparalleled battery longevity. Its seamless integration of these features makes it a standout option in the market, earning it the title of the easiest laptop to recommend for those seeking a blend of performance and convenience.

For users prioritizing portability without compromising on performance, the MacBook Air M3 emerges as an exceptional solution. Its feather-light construction makes it effortless to carry around, whether for work on-the-go or casual browsing at home. Despite its slim profile, this laptop packs a punch with its robust processing capabilities, ensuring smooth multitasking and efficient handling of everyday tasks.

Typing enthusiasts will find solace in the MacBook Air M3's keyboard design, which offers a tactile and responsive typing experience. Whether composing lengthy emails, drafting documents, or engaging in creative pursuits, users can rely on the comfort and accuracy facilitated by the laptop's keyboard, enhancing productivity and reducing strain during extended typing sessions.

Moreover, the MacBook Air M3 boasts category-leading battery life, providing users with extended periods of uninterrupted usage. This exceptional battery performance enhances the laptop's appeal, allowing users to tackle their tasks without the constant need for recharging. Ultimately, for individuals seeking a well-rounded laptop experience tailored to work-casual usage, the MacBook Air M3 emerges as a standout choice, earning its reputation as the easiest recommendation in its class.

ABOUT THE AUTHOR

Perry Hoover is a researcher, tech Entrepreneur, blogger and a technology writer, who is fond of blogging, technology research and writing. His areas of interest include Web application penetration testing, web security/architecture, cryptography, programming languages and database security. He is well versed with the latest technology, programming languages, computer hardware/software, and programming tools. He is also an expert in database security and application security architecture and penetration testing. He loves to share information about new technology and has published dozens of articles on it.

He has written articles on different aspects of IT Technologies including IT security, data storage and application development for magazines and has also published and co-published several e-books, of which the latest is on Windows 11. He has also worked with different private agencies to provide solutions to IT problems.

Printed in Dunstable, United Kingdom

64213120R00157